Social Issues
in Literature

War in Joseph Heller's
Catch-22

Other Books in the Social Issues in Literature Series:

Social Issues
in Literature

War in Joseph Heller's
Catch-22

Dedria Bryfonski, Book Editor

GREENHAVEN PRESS
A part of Gale, Cengage Learning

Detroit • New York • San Francisco • New Haven, Conn • Waterville, Maine • London

GALE
CENGAGE Learning

Christine Nasso, *Publisher*
Elizabeth Des Chenes, *Managing Editor*

© 2009 Greenhaven Press, a part of Gale, Cengage Learning

Gale and Greenhaven Press are registered trademarks used herein under license.

For more information, contact:
Greenhaven Press
27500 Drake Rd.
Farmington Hills, MI 48331-3535
Or you can visit our Internet site at gale.cengage.com

For product information and technology assistance, contact us at

Gale Customer Support, 1-800-877-4253
For permission to use material from this text or product, submit all requests online at www.cengage.com/permissions

Further permissions questions can be emailed to permissionrequest@cengage.com

Articles in Greenhaven Press anthologies are often edited for length to meet page requirements. In addition, original titles of these works are changed to clearly present the main thesis and to explicitly indicate the author's opinion. Every effort is made to ensure that Greenhaven Press accurately reflects the original intent of the authors. Every effort has been made to trace the owners of copyrighted material.

Cover image by Getty Images.

LIBRARY OF CONGRESS CATALOGING-IN-PUBLICATION DATA

War in Joseph Heller's Catch-22 / Dedria Bryfonski, book editor.
    p. cm. -- (Social issues in literature)
    Includes bibliographical references and index.
    ISBN 978-0-7377-4400-2
    ISBN 978-0-7377-4399-9 (pbk.)
    1. Heller, Joseph. Catch-22. 2. War in literature. 3. World War, 1939-1945--Literature and the war. I. Bryfonski, Dedria.
    PS3558.E476C3388 2009
    813'.54--dc22

                                                                2009003280

Printed in the United States of America
1 2 3 4 5 6 7 13 12 11 10 09

Contents

Chapter 1: Background on Joseph Heller

Heller was a master satirist who used humor to depict the horrors of war and the intrusion of bureaucracy into the government and military. The title of his first novel and best-known work, *Catch-22*, has entered the American lexicon to mean a "bureaucratic paradox," in which the only solution is made impossible by a rule inherent in the problem itself.

Heller's father died suddenly when Heller was five years old, an event that shaped the author's life. Death was Heller's major subject, and he approached it with gallows humor.

In both his life and his fiction, Heller takes a satiric look at the way in which comedy and tragedy interact.

On the American political scene in the early 1960s, the passivity of the Eisenhower years was giving way to the vigor of the Kennedy years. During that period, American writing similarly changed. *Catch-22* was the first novel of the movement that would come to be called postmodernism.

Chapter 2: *Catch-22* and War

Chapter 3: Contemporary Perspectives on War

Introduction

In one of the ironies of modern literature, a close examination of *Catch-22* reveals it is not really the antiwar bible claimed by 1960s Vietnam War protesters. In numerous interviews, Heller makes it clear that he supported World War II, which he fought in and writes about in *Catch-22*. The final speech of the book's main character, John Yossarian, has been cited by many reviewers as weakening the novel, for they consider it out of synch with the antiwar sentiments of the rest of the book. The distinction made by Yossarian in his speech, however, is entirely consistent with Heller's own professed sentiments about the war. As Yossarian says to Major Danby:

> I earned that medal I got, no matter what their reasons were for giving it to me. I've flown seventy goddam combat missions. Don't talk to me about fighting to save my country. I've been fighting all along to save my country. Now I'm going to fight a little to save myself. The country's not in danger any more, but I am.

What is rarely noted by critics who have trouble with this passage is the fact that Yossarian is attempting to escape from active duty only at the end of the war, when the outcome is assured. He was willing to fly combat missions at the beginning of the war to save his country. It is only at the war's denouement, with victory in sight, that his instincts for self-preservation lead him to various ways to escape more combat—combat he sees as simply supporting the self-serving goals of those in command.

In an interview in the *Realist*, Heller emphasizes this point: "I also tried to make it very evident that the war was just about over.... But if you postulate *this* situation: It's right after Pearl Harbor, and we *don't* have enough planes, and we *don't* have enough men, and Hitler *is* in a dominant and threatening position, then it would be a completely different situation."

Such a reading is consistent with comments Heller has made about his own feelings about World War II. Speaking to Sam Merrill in an interview that appeared in *Playboy* in 1975, Heller says, "I still feel [World War II] was a necessary war. *Catch-22* was criticized because Yossarian justifies his participation in World War II until the outcome is no longer in doubt. It offended some people, during the Vietnam War, that I had not written a truly pacifist book. But I am not a true pacifist. World War II was necessary at least to the extent that we were fighting for the survival of millions of people."

Heller echoed these sentiments in 1981, in an interview with Chet Filippo for *Rolling Stone* in which he said, "I've been criticized for my ending, for my not being a pacifist and for Yossarian's failure to condemn [World War II]. But these readers wanted something far beyond anything I was willing to say or feel about World War II—that *any* alternative is preferable to war. That's *not* my attitude, and it's not expressed *anywhere* in the book."

If *Catch-22* is not an antiwar novel, then what is Heller criticizing? Readers can look to why Yossarian wants to escape—he is afraid that his own superiors are trying to kill him and considers himself more at risk from his own military than from the Germans. Heller has stated on several occasions that the real enemy in *Catch-22* is the military, that people are in danger from their own government. To drive home his theme, Heller satirizes bureaucracy, patriotism, loyalty oaths, and the free-enterprise system. *Catch-22* is, as he has said, more about the Cold War and the Vietnam War than it is about World War II. Heller says he set *Catch-22* during World War II "because I knew World War II." However, it was not published until 1961, and the bureaucratic spirit of the Cold War is much more a part of its sensibility than the patriotism of World War II.

In the essays in this volume, critics examine the extent of Heller's pacifism and discuss the various events in recent American history to which *Catch-22* relates, as well as addressing several other topics. In addition, a number of viewpoints offer contemporary perspectives on war, focusing particularly on government policies regarding the Iraq War.

Chronology

1923

Joseph Heller is born on May 1 in the Coney Island section of Brooklyn, New York, to Isaac and Lena Heller, Jewish immigrants from Russia.

1927

Isaac Heller dies from a botched operation.

1941

Heller graduates from Abraham Lincoln High School in the Flatbush section of Brooklyn and takes a job as a file clerk in an insurance office.

1942

Following the United States's entry into World War II, Heller takes a job as a blacksmith's helper at the Norfolk Navy Yard. After a short time, he enlists in the army air corps and enrolls in cadet school.

1944

Heller completes his training as a bombardier. He is assigned to the 488th Squadron of the Twelfth Air Force stationed in Corsica. He flies sixty missions over Italy and France as a wing bombardier.

1945

Upon his honorable discharge as a first lieutenant from the army, Heller is awarded an Air Medal and a Presidential Unit Citation. He marries Shirley Held and enrolls in the University of Southern California on the G.I. Bill. His first story, "I Don't Love You Anymore," is published by *Story* magazine.

1946

Heller transfers to New York University. He is encouraged in his writing by Maurice Baudin, whose course on short-story composition Heller took.

1948

Heller graduates Phi Beta Kappa from New York University. He has four short stories published—two in *Esquire* and two in *Atlantic Monthly*.

1949

Heller receives his master's degree in English from Columbia University and studies English literature at St. Catherine's College, Oxford University, on a Fulbright Scholarship.

1950

Returning from England, Heller teaches English composition at Pennsylvania State College, where he collaborates on a movie script with other faculty members.

1952

A daughter, Erica, is born to Shirley and Joseph Heller. Heller takes a job as advertising copywriter at *Time* magazine.

1955

"The Texan" is published in *New World Writing*, the first chapter of a war novel he was then calling *Catch-18*.

1956

Heller's son, Theodore, is born. Heller moves to *Look* magazine as an advertising promotion writer.

1957

Simon and Schuster offers Heller a contract for his war novel.

1958

Heller moves to *McCall's* magazine.

1959

Heller's short story "McAdam's Log" appears in *Gentleman's Quarterly*.

1961

Catch-22 is published and sells thirty-two thousand copies in its first year.

1962

The movie rights to *Catch-22* are sold to Columbia Pictures. Heller leaves his job at *McCall's* and writes a script for the TV pilot of *McHale's Navy*.

1963

Heller is awarded a National Institute of Arts and Letters grant in literature.

1964

Heller turns to full-time writing and completes a screenplay for *Sex and the Single Girl*.

1966

The first chapter of *Something Happened* is published in *Esquire*.

1967

Heller teaches creative writing classes at the University of Pennsylvania and, later, Yale University, where he would also be playwright-in-residence. His play *We Bombed in New Haven* is produced by Yale School of Drama Repertory Theater.

1968

We Bombed in New Haven opens in New York and runs for eleven weeks. The play is published by Knopf.

1970

The film version of *Catch-22* is released.

1971

Heller writes a dramatization of *Catch-22* and the play is produced in East Hampton, New York. He becomes Distinguished Visiting Professor at the City College of New York (CCNY).

1973

Clevinger's Trial, a one-act play, is published by Samuel R. French.

1974

Something Happened is published by Knopf.

1975

Heller gives up his teaching position at CCNY to write full time.

1979

Good as Gold is published by Simon and Schuster.

1981

Heller separates from his wife, Shirley. He comes down with Guillain-Barré syndrome in December.

1982

During a lengthy recuperation from his disease, Heller meets Valerie Humphries, a nurse.

1984

The Hellers are divorced. *God Knows* is published by Knopf.

1986

With his friend Speed Vogel, Heller coauthors *No Laughing Matter*, the story of his illness. It is published by G.P. Putnam's Sons.

1987

Heller and Valerie Humphries are married.

1988
Picture This is published by G.P. Putnam's Sons.

1991
Heller lectures at Oxford University on a Christensen Fellowship.

1994
Closing Time: A Novel, the sequel to *Catch 22*, is published by Simon and Schuster.

1998
Now and Then: From Coney Island to Here, Heller's autobiography, is published by Simon and Schuster.

1999
Heller dies of a heart attack in December at the age of seventy-six.

2000
Portrait of the Artist as an Old Man is published posthumously by Simon and Schuster.

2003
Catch as Catch Can: The Collected Stories and Other Writings is published by Simon and Schuster.

Social Issues
in Literature

CHAPTER 1

| Background on
Joseph Heller

The Life of Joseph Heller

David Seed

David Seed is a lecturer in English at the University of Liver-pool. He is the author or editor of numerous books and articles about American and English writers, including The Fiction of Joseph Heller: Against the Grain.

David Seed, in the following excerpts, discusses Heller as a groundbreaking figure in American literature who introduced satire and humor to the genre of war fiction and added a new phrase, "catch-22," to the American lexicon. Seed suggests that Heller's upbringing in Coney Island (Brooklyn, New York) may be responsible for the comic aspects of his fiction and traces several central themes throughout the works of Heller, including the search for a missing father and the fear of death.

Joseph Heller has established himself as a major satirist in the field of contemporary American fiction. A new phrase was added to the American lexicon from the title of his first novel, *Catch-22* (1961). The term "catch-22" has become accepted in *Webster's New World Dictionary* and the *Oxford English Dictionary* and denotes a bureaucratic paradox, having the effect of entrapping the subject. Heller's fiction continues to be examined for its use of absurdist techniques and more recently for its critique of Cold War America. Heller was elected to the American Academy of Letters in 1977; in 1985 he was awarded two French prizes: the Prix Médicis Étranger and the Prix Interallié.

David Seed, "Joseph Heller," in *Dictionary of Literary Biography, vol. 227, American Novelists Since World War II, Sixth Series*, Farmington Hills, MI: The Gale Group, 2000, pp. 184–204. Copyright © 2000 Gale Group. Reproduced by permission of Gale, a part of Cengage Learning.

Father's Early Death and Coney Island Upbringing Are Formative

Joseph Heller was born in Brooklyn, New York, to Russian Jewish immigrants, Isaac Heller, a truck driver, and Lena Heller, on 1 May 1923. He had a basically secular upbringing, his mother being more concerned with social forms than religious observance. His father died as a result of a bungled operation when Heller was five, and his friend and journalist Barbara Gelb feels that this event caused a psychic wound, revealing itself in the recurrence of death as a central focus in Heller's writing. Looking back on the Coney Island neighborhood where his family lived, Heller has always recalled those years with nostalgia, and indeed the Coney Island Luna Park must have had a formative influence on Heller's perception of comic spectacle and the streetwise banter of the showmen. In his 1962 article "Coney Island: The Fun Is Over" Heller recorded his memories of the barkers who created a "setup where the customer could never win." The confidence tricks recur on a small scale within different contexts in Heller's novels.

In his youth Heller was an avid reader of Jerome Weidman's fiction of New York's Lower East Side. At the age of thirteen, he briefly held a job as a Western Union messenger boy, an experience he drew on for his 1962 story "World Full of Great Cities." In his teens he tried his hand at writing short stories while holding brief jobs as a file clerk in a casualty insurance company, a blacksmith's helper in a naval yard, and a shipping file clerk. In 1942 Heller joined the U.S. Army Air Corps and from May 1944 to mid 1945 was stationed on Corsica with the 488th squadron of the 340th Bombardment Group. He flew about sixty combat missions as a bombardier, earning the Air Medal and rising to the rank of lieutenant. The 37th mission over Avignon proved to be one of the most dangerous and was later written into *Catch-22* in the descriptions of Snowden's death.

On his discharge from the air corps Heller married Shirley Held and enrolled at the University of Southern California under the G.I. Bill, but with the help of Whit Burnett, the editor of *Story* magazine, he transferred to New York University. New York has remained Heller's preferred location partly because of the tempo of life and partly because—as he wisecracked in a press conference—the people are so unfriendly. Heller's first published work, "I Don't Love You Any More," was an account of a returned soldier, which came out in the servicemen's issue of *Story* in 1945. Heller's letters from this period suggest that Burnett played an important part in encouraging his writing, as did Maurice Baudin, whose course on short story composition Heller took at New York University. "Baudin pointed out my faults to me," Heller has recalled. "He'd say throw away the first three or four pages, and he was right." Although it is generally thought that *Catch-22* was written entirely in the 1950s, as early as 1945 Heller was considering a novel about a "flier facing the end of his missions and thinking over the meaning of the war." Heller's earliest short stories are characterized by the pattern of satiric realism encouraged by periodicals such as *Esquire*. He graduated Phi Beta Kappa in 1948 and during the following year took an M.A. at Columbia University where his professors included Lionel Trilling. In 1949 he received a Fulbright scholarship to St. Catherine's College, Oxford, where, according to his fellow student Edward J. Bloustein, he spent much of his time working on short stories. In 1991 Heller returned to Oxford as a Christensen Visiting Fellow and that same year was elected to an Honorary Fellowship of St. Catherine's.

On his return to the United States he accepted a post as an English instructor at what was then Pennsylvania State College. Finding the place and the teaching uncongenial, Heller left Penn State in 1952 to join *Time* magazine as an advertising copywriter until 1956, when he moved on to *Look*, and then served as promotion manager at *McCall's* from 1958 to

Joseph Heller Michael A. Smith/Time Life Pictures/Getty Images.

1961. All of this commercial experience fed directly into his second novel *Something Happened* (1974). Two stories that stand out from Heller's pre-*Catch-22* years as showing signs of future promise are "World Full of Great Cities" (written 1947, published 1962) and "MacAdam's Log" (written 1950, published 1959). . . .

Early Reviewers Misunderstand *Catch-22*

[When *Catch-18*, as Heller's classic was originally called,] was on the verge of publication in 1961, Heller's editor decided the title would have to be changed because Leon Uris's novel *Mila 18* was scheduled for the same year. Heller came up with the number 22, which actually captures more effectively the motif of duplication. Despite an elaborate promotional campaign, *Catch-22* was slow to sell at first, faring better in Britain. Some reviewers were openly hostile, such as Whitney Balliett in *The New Yorker* complaining that the book gives the impression of having been "shouted onto paper." One of the problems faced by Heller was the lack of preparedness in the reviewers for the unorthodox experimentalism of the work. Heller attacks not only the institutionalized authority of the military but also the conventional decorum of novelistic realism. Accordingly, his novel could be usefully compared with the works of other dark humorists of the 1960s, writers such as Philip Roth and Bruce Jay Friedman, who outraged their readers by bawdily ridiculing Jewish stereotypes, or with Terry Southern, who deployed an anarchic humor against such targets as evangelism and the pornographic movie business. These works characteristically used urban locations, fast-moving and increasingly ludicrous plots, and a humor that respected no sacred cows. The hostility of some reviewers, therefore, represented their anger at seeing their preconceptions challenged. In interviews Heller has explained how he was drawn to novelists such as Evelyn Waugh and Vladimir Nabokov, who apparently invert the relation between triviality and importance found in other works.

At every point *Catch-22* questions the conventions of the American war novel. It includes a farcical reprise of the lake journey to freedom in Ernest Hemingway's *A Farewell To Arms* (1929) when Orr rows to Sweden. While James Jones used the army to represent the stratifications of American society, Heller uses it to demonstrate the paranoia of the McCarthy era. . . . The main sequence designated by the novel's title is a circular one. Catch-22 consists of a juncture between two propositions where the conditions of one contradict or disable the other. Insanity would be one basis for obtaining relief from bombing missions, but the official entailment that this be requested in writing is prima facie proof of the applicant's sanity. The result of this double bind is to entrap the officers and to preserve intact the obligation to go on the missions. In that sense Catch-22 becomes symptomatic of officialdom's independence of rational scrutiny. As more and more instances occur in the novel, the title phrase comes to represent a sinister principle at work behind the scenes rather than an individual clause. One condition of Catch-22 is that its existence does not have to be demonstrated, with the result that it comes to signal the operation of an authoritarian, if lunatic, administration. . . .

This self-perpetuating bureaucratic logic is one of the key imperatives in *Catch-22*, others being the profit motive (embodied in Milo) and the need for an enemy. The latter suggests yet another reason why some reviewers were so disconcerted when the novel first appeared. For *Catch-22* presents a hybrid fiction where World War II is merged into the McCarthy era. Heller has stated in interviews, how distressed he has been to witness that the military "retains its enormous influence on affairs in a peacetime situation" and accordingly has deployed anachronisms that make it impossible to limit the events of the book to 1944–1945. The repetition of cuewords like "subversive" by the leading paranoids in the novel, the loyalty oath campaign, and above all the extended interrogation of the chaplain all evoke the political atmosphere of the early 1950s, which was when Heller began work in earnest on *Catch-22*. Drawing partly on Franz Kafka's novel *The Trial* (1937), Heller has stated that in the interrogation he was trying to capture the atmosphere of the congressional hearings; he also found a suggestive similarity between his own novel and Richard Condon's account of conspiracy in *The Manchurian Candidate* (1959). Both novels, he told *The Realist*, "are at once serious and at the same time it's almost like watching a kind of burlesque." . . .

Heller Writes for the Theater

For years Heller had been interested in the theater. . . . As soon as *Catch-22* was published, Paul Newman invited Heller to consider working with the members of the Actors Studio on adaptations from the novel; Heller declined. During a visit to Yale University in December 1966, Heller mentioned the idea of a dramatic adaptation to Robert Brustein, dean of the Yale Drama School. Brustein was enthusiastic and helped secure Heller a temporary appointment at Yale; Brustein had transformed the drama school into an important location for the theater of protest against the Vietnam War. By this time the commercial success of *Catch-22* had enabled Heller to leave his job at *McCall's*.

Heller's play *We Bombed in New Haven* was first produced at Yale in 1967 and is a work that constantly disrupts the theatrical illusion, the curtain half-rising as if in error to reveal the actors still getting ready for the production. Virtually all the action takes place in an air force briefing room where the Major carries papers doubling as military orders and as the script of the play itself. Heller's plan was to use this device to raise questions about the actors' free will: "Can they break away from the script?" Gaps were left in the script that the actors could fill with improvisations depending on the audience's responses. The play's title links theatrical failure with military combat, and the dialogue moves in and out of different levels of reality (war-as-theater, war-as-game) to prevent the audience ever losing their awareness of watching a stage production. The play draws on *King Lear* to develop a relatively minor motif in *Catch-22*, the relation of parents to children. Major Starkey in effect plays the role of a deity in deciding which figures (always *young* ones) are expendable. The disconcerting formality of the dialogue between Starkey and his son reflects their total estrangement from each other, and in his

1995 study Stephen W. Potts correctly suggested that the Vietnam War was widely perceived to be a collective betrayal of sons by fathers.

We Bombed in New Haven includes many allusions to other wars, but the common consciousness of the Vietnam War must have been paramount in 1967. By the end of that decade *Catch-22* had established itself as the novel with the most pointed and parodistic relevance to that war. In the play Heller achieves the dislocation of language from reality by having a character declare: "There is no war taking place," only to have his words interrupted by an explosion. At another point a plastic time bomb is thrown into the audience, simultaneously drawing them into the situation of warfare and warning that for America time is running out. As in *Catch-22* the concept of "enemy" is revised and relocated so that Americans are shown to be killing fellow Americans. . . .

After its publication, the movie rights to *Catch-22* were bought by Columbia Pictures, who then hired Heller to write the screenplay, but Heller had so little interest in this undertaking that he waived his contractual rights. [American writer, actor, and director] Buck Henry was next asked to write the screen adaptation, which Henry showed to Heller before filming started. Heller expressed mixed feelings about the script and the finished movie, noting with regret the disappearance of the crucial interrogation scenes, changes to characters, and the use of gratuitous comic effects. On the other hand, he did praise the depiction of Snowden's slow death and what he called the "philosophical weariness" of the old woman in the brothel. . . .

Heller Writes Three More Novels

Heller's second novel, *Something Happened*, was originally planned to have a much stronger continuity with *Catch-22* than the finished novel displayed. A preliminary sketch published in 1966 under the same title identifies its narrator/

protagonist as a former bombardier who has flown missions over Italy and France. These details were removed from the novel, which plays down the importance of wartime memories. *Something Happened* consists of an extended monologue by business executive Bob Slocum, who is going through extended midlife doldrums. . . .

Good as Gold (1979) partly returns to the parodic methods of *Catch-22* in describing how its protagonist Bruce Gold fluctuates between two worlds: the Jewish context of his family and the political world of Washington, D.C. Heller set out to produce a tongue-in-cheek account of the "Jewish Experience in America" and paints an unflattering but hilarious portrait of the antagonisms running through Gold's family. . . .

Heller based his next novel, *God Knows* (1984), on the biblical story of David. Although the book immediately became a best-seller, many of the reviews were hostile, drawing comparisons with the comic monologue, "The Two Thousand-Year-Old Man," by Heller's longtime friend, [American actor, comedian, director, and writer] Mel Brooks. Despite its superficial divergence from Heller's usual preference for contemporary subjects, this novel bears a close thematic relevance to his other works through the related issues of authority and justice. One of the central problems in *God Knows* lies in David's relation to his two symbolic fathers, Saul and God. In *Catch-22* Heller had engaged with this relationship, presenting Major Major Major as the victim of a black joke played on him by his father. The protagonist of *Good as Gold* suffers endless torments at the hands of his sadistic father, and when the death of his elder brother leaves Gold notionally as the head of his family, he is saddled with two parents who reject their relation to him. The position of fathers in the Jewish tradition is absolutely central and bound up with questions of religion and assimilation.

David was an unusual but logical choice for Heller, because in a sense he had three fathers—Jesse, Saul, and God—and lost them all. . . .

Heller Is Stricken with Guillain-Barré Syndrome

In December 1981, while in the middle of writing *God Knows*, Heller was suddenly struck down by a serious disease that attacks the nervous system, Guillain-Barré Syndrome, which for a time paralyzed him completely. He later published an account of his ordeal, cowritten by his friend Speed Vogel, in *No Laughing Matter* (1986). Heller describes the worst stage of his illness as a figurative descent into hell where he felt the "mortal dread" of succumbing to an urge to sleep that would be his last. Once he had recovered, a second difficulty emerged: Heller had repeatedly stated his dislike for the factual precision needed in nonfiction. During his illness he was given a copy of Norman Cousins's *Anatomy of an Illness* (1979) that describes a process of self-therapy administered during a disease of the connective tissues. *No Laughing Matter* bears little resemblance to this work since Heller was content to be a relatively passive patient. What was much more important to him was his capacity to speak, which restored his contact with the outside world. Vogel's chapters were written first, and then Heller produced his own. The result is a good-humored dialogue between friends who sometimes give contrasting versions of the same event, and a narrative that also reveals the differences between what Heller experienced and what those around him saw. Death is either referred to in a matter-of-fact way or defused by comedy, as when Vogel writes a pastiche sentimental account of Heller dying in his arms. There are three subplots to *No Laughing Matter*: the comedy of Mel Brooks's interference with the hospital authorities, the drawn-out legal wrangling of Heller's divorce, and the growing love between himself and his nurse, Valerie Humphries, whom he married a year after the book was published.

With the passing of his illness Heller experienced a new surge of productivity, completing *God Knows* writing his chapters of *No Laughing Matter*, and publishing articles on his illness. In addition he started his next novel, *Picture This* (1988), which has proved more difficult to assess than any of his other works. The book has a double subject—Rembrandt and seventeenth-century Dutch culture, and the history of Athens from the Peloponnesian War (431–404 b.c.) to the death of Socrates (399 b.c.). Structurally the two periods are linked by an artifact—Rembrandt's painting *Aristotle Contemplating a Bust of Homer* (1653). From Gary Schwartz's 1985 biography *Rembrandt: His Life, His Paintings*, Heller took the model of tracing out the painter's relation to patrons. He drew also on Simon Schama's massive book *The Embarrassment of Riches: An Interpretation of Dutch Culture in the Golden Age* (1987), which relates painting and other cultural activities to the newly independent Netherlands' desire for self-legitimation. (The Netherlands' independence from Spanish rule was enacted by the Treaty of Westphalia in 1648.). . .

Closing Time Is Sequel to *Catch-22*

Closing Time (1994) was publicized as the long-awaited sequel to *Catch-22*; though it continues and revises many motifs from the earlier novel, the new work replaces a uniform absurdism with a mixed mode, combining satire with surrealism. Heller focuses on different dimensions of time, especially in relation to the ultimate ending of death. To highlight the latter theme, the cover of the first edition portrayed black figures silhouetted in the dance of death. The novel is saturated with references to time and repeatedly privileges the act of remembering, starting from the opening chapter, where Sammy Singer, a wartime friend of Yossarian's, looks back through old photographs and mementos. For the main characters of *Clos-*

ing Time, most things have already happened. Sammy remembers his grandfather being mocked for his World War I regalia, but the novel positions itself, partly through Sammy's memories, at an historical moment where the generation that has lived through World War II—Heller's own, in other words—is on the verge of extinction. The more recent war will also recede into an anonymous past; "soon . . . there will be no more of us left," Sammy reflects. Time is valued as a rare commodity about to run out. . . .

In *Closing Time* Heller partly mounts an extended reexamination of his own youth. *Now and Then: From Coney Island to Here* (1998) completes this process by documenting further the importance Coney Island had for him as spectacle and as an early education against expecting value for money. This memoir fills out the information on Heller's early reading that previously had only been available in scattered interviews. His favorite authors included the humorists Robert Benchley and P.G. Wodehouse, and the realists who offered models for his own first stories, Irwin Shaw and William Saroyan. The memoir also sheds new light on Heller's own satirical interests when he records his enthusiasm for H.L. Mencken's attacks on "hokum." Looking back on his life, Heller quietly identifies a recurring tendency to "stifle painful emotion"; *Now and Then* reverses this denial by his recalling of all those events where he came close to death: swimming out to the Coney Island bell for example, or almost having his fingers sheared in a blacksmith's shop. Heller's memoir completes a process of self-examination that had begun decades ago with personality tests (alerting him to the countless reminders of mortality in *Catch-22*) and periods of psychotherapy. Above all, *Now and Then* reinstates the figure of the missing father who has recurred throughout Heller's writing and who is now recognized: "I know him by his absence." This understated autobiography makes an excellent companion to Heller's fiction, in its commentary on the central themes of his novels and its account of origins.

Heller Dies in 1999

Joseph Heller died of a heart attack on 12 December 1999 at the age of seventy-six. Throughout his almost forty years as a novelist, Heller used humor and satire to give expression to the horrors of war and to a distrust of bureaucracy and government that reached its peak during the Vietnam War. His fiction radically altered a whole generation of readers' perception of America.

Friend and fellow novelist Kurt Vonnegut spoke for that generation in describing Joseph Heller's death as a "calamity for American letters." At the time of his death, Heller left a completed novel titled "Portrait of the Artist as an Old Man."

Death Is a Central Subject for Heller

Barbara Gelb

Barbara Gelb has written several books and magazine articles. Among her best-known books are O'Neill: Life with Monte Cristo, *coauthored with her husband, Arthur Gelb, and* So Short a Time: A Biography of John Reed and Louise Bryant.

In this personal essay, Barbara Gelb reveals that her friend Joseph Heller is beset by many demons. She claims he is fixated on his own mortality, his health, and his anxieties about the creative process. She attributes his fear of death to his father's having died at an early age but notes that Heller's response to fear, however, is to laugh in the face of pain and suffering.

To Joseph Heller, death has always been a laughing matter. He was 5 when his father died suddenly, and he remembers the day of the funeral as a party. He was petted and crooned to and fed cake and candy. He was considered too young to understand grief, and for years he never heard his father's death mentioned, nor did he ask. Twenty-five years later, having confronted his own death on 60 missions as a bombardier in World War II, he began writing *Catch-22*, the funny and shocking novel about death in war that was to turn him, after the book's completion eight years later, into an aging prodigy.

Laughing in the Face of Death

Some writers are born to the tragic view and learn to embrace it, saying, as Eugene O'Neill did, "Life is a tragedy, hurrah!" Others, like Heller, acknowledge the tragedy, but hold it at

Barbara Gelb, "Catching Joseph Heller," *New York Times Magazine*, March 4, 1979, pp. 14–16, 42, 44, 46, 48, 51–52, 54–55. Copyright © 1979 by The New York Times Company. Reprinted with permission.

arm's length, laughing in its face. (Death is a party, ha ha.) Heller grew up with this odd and isolating concept. His mother would chide him, in response to an oblique joke, "You have a twisted brain." And it was no more than the truth. Grimacing, Heller chose to nourish the twist and perfect the strangled laugh. His joke is the comedy of despair.

Heller continues to laugh about death. The joke is at the core of all of his writings—his long second novel, *Something Happened*, his play, *We Bombed in New Haven*, and his . . . third novel, *Good as Gold*. In all four of his works [as of 1979], death is present as an event and a foreboding. In each, the climax is precipitated by the death of someone close to the protagonist—who always survives, gasping with gratitude.

Readers in the millions have laughed with pain and recognition at his wicked social satire, and have moaned (a favorite Heller verb) over the wayward wretchedness of his trapped non-heroes; literary critics here and abroad applaud his daring and his ferocity, analyze the gallows-grimness of his comedy and often, in passing, chide him for his languor and the paucity of his *oeuvre.* . . .

Hard to Get to Know

Outside the solitude of his writing, he is a largely hidden man, locked into a pose of tempered bellicosity (sometimes not so tempered); he masks his feelings with mockery and laughter. In this pose he can at times be extremely entertaining. He can also turn offensive. It is dismaying to realize that the pose is intended to conceal a dreadful malaise. Only his immediate family and a handful of intimate friends are aware of the seething feelings that Heller prefers not to examine— that, in fact, he denies exist. He really believes in the magic of denial.

Throughout his life, Heller has been spinning himself a cocoon, layer over layer. This enables him to joke not only about death, but about all the other phantoms waiting to pounce, the instant he lowers his guard. He worries a lot about heart attacks, strokes and cancer. He is nearly 56 and his friends are dying. A compulsive dieter and jogger, who quit smoking 25 years ago, he has slid into his midlife crisis, biting his nails ("nibbling and gnawing away aggressively, swinishly, and vengefully at my own finger tips," whines the deliciously craven Slocum in *Something Happened*).

Heller fears the loss of his talent. He fears to embrace his fame or to dissipate his money. (He believes he will never have another idea for a novel, that he will be left destitute in his old age and that he will be introduced to someone who will not recognize his name.) He fears the emotional commitment of love and is embarrassed to feel any such stirring.

"I can let myself feel for people and I can let myself stop feeling for them," he says, quite sincerely. "It's easy, it's a skill—like an ability to draw."

Heller's Love for His Dog

Some people find Heller prickly and forbidding. If they were dogs, they would understand the tenderness below the surface. Dogs adore him; he lavished his love on pets until his second dog, a sweet-faced Bedlington terrier named Sweeney, died of cancer [in 1977]. If you are not a dog, it takes patience and perseverance to discover Heller's tenderness, I met him [in 1974] and it has taken me all this time to begin to understand the cause and source of his shielding laughter.

It happened that Heller and his wife, Shirley, to whom he has been married for 33 years, were coming to dinner on the day that Sweeney's illness was diagnosed as fatal and the decision made to put the dog to sleep. Heller, who knew I loved *Something Happened*, had by then begun to include me among the half dozen or so of his friends to whom he showed bits of his work in progress. I had him eating out of my hand when I mentioned that I had been struck by his novel's evocation of O'Neill's *Long Day's Journey Into Night*—a cruelly *funny Long*

Day's Journey, but nonetheless weighty, as the play is with guilts and ghosts and paternal sin.

When Shirley Heller called to explain about Sweeney and say she and Joe would be late for dinner, I remembered an evening a few months earlier when I had been a guest of the Hellers. He had cradled Sweeney in his arms as he saw me out on that occasion, and I was astonished when he held up the dog's paw and said, in dulcet tones (to the dog), "Wave good-bye to Auntie Babawa, Sweeney baby."

But even his love of dogs is not sacred. He will turn a joke against himself, just as readily as taunt his worst enemy or best friend. Once, during Sweeney's reign, Shirley Heller, who is her husband's most appreciative audience (and sometimes his crooked straight man), suggested going to a romantic movie that was being advertised with the invitation "See it with someone you love." Heller grinned wickedly. "I'd like to," he said, "but I'm afraid they won't let me in with Sweeney." It is Shirley Heller who tells this story. She is as adept as her husband at self-mockery.

The evening Sweeney's fate was sealed, the Hellers arrived at my apartment looking glum. Shirley appeared stricken even as she was laughing at her husband's wisecracks. She is the only person I've ever known who can laugh and cry at the same time, and is, therefore, the perfect Heller heroine. As for Heller, he told me later, "I broke down in the vet's office, inconsolably and uncontrollably." He forswore ever owning another pet. He had devoted a lot of time to walking Sweeney and grooming him, and there is now another small hollow in his life.

Heller's buffed feelings are so fragile, his nerve ends so raw, he can survive only by trying to fool himself: What you don't know can't hurt you. It is a documented neurosis and it stems from his childhood. His talent for abnegation has been a matter of mild concern to his friends for years.

Small Circle of Close Friends

"I never knew anybody so determined to be unhappy, so suspicious of happiness," [American writer] Mario Puzo says. Puzo, one of Heller's longtime friends, grew up Italian in Manhattan's Hell's Kitchen, rather than Jewish in Coney Island, as Heller did. But he shares with Heller an impoverished, immigrant background and the resultant street smarts and street scars.

"Joe is afraid to be happy; if he's happy, he gets unhappy," Puzo says. "Control over his feelings is important to him. He's so concerned about controlling his life, he can't have fun. Actually, I can even see him changing into a wild man, but it would be in a very controlled sort of way."

Puzo was thinking of the sort of outrageous (but just within the bounds of safety) behavior Heller sometimes indulges in. Once, at a cocktail party (to which Heller had gone with a friend reluctantly), he introduced himself to a couple of doctors as a fellow physician who specialized in geriatric illnesses. Heller, who reads everything about health, had been boning up on the subject as a hedge against his own imminent disintegration (imminent ever since he turned 30, calculated that his life was half over, and began to fear he had no future). He challenged the doctors knowledgeably, declaring, among other things: "If you study Menninger on mitosis, you foretell diagnosis." He was not quite convincing enough and the doctors began to feel affronted.

Sometimes, seeing that he is being taken amiss, Heller stops in time. On other occasions he either does not recognize the hostility he is incurring, or chooses to ignore it. In this case, the friend with whom he had gone to the party stepped in protectively and explained to Heller's victims that "Joe is just kidding; it's the way he is with everyone."

Heller did not miss a beat. "I make such efforts to alienate people," he said, still speaking to his boiling victims, "and this guy [his friend] comes along, wipes out all the bad will I've created." He walked away, laughing.

He was up to the same tricks as long as 30 years ago, when he was a Fulbright Scholar at Oxford, along with another ex-G.I., Edward Bloustein. Bloustein, now [in 1979] the president of Rutgers University, recalls that Heller "was then as he is now."

"I had a distinct sense of the strength of this guy, the compulsion for perfection, his attitude toward language," he says. "Joe was sometimes amusing and often sardonic. But he had and has a very biting humor that sometimes distresses me. His humor is delivered so deadpan, people misinterpret it and can feel insulted. This happened often when I was with him in England. I would take the people aside and explain Joe to them, and then they would find him the attractive man he is."

Heller forces himself to socialize—sometimes to help the sale of his books, sometimes out of boredom—and it is possible for him, aided by two or three martinis, to have much fun on such occasions. What he prefers, though, is the conversation of his friends, particularly if they are on his own wavelength of outrageous and ribald humor. Mel Brooks, the movie man and sometime friend, says, "Joe plays the best verbal Ping-Pong of anyone I know. The ball will be returned with a spin on it, always. He has a Talmudic tenacity in argument."

But he is a closet recluse. He sees the same old friends week after week, never seeming to tire of the basically boring, second-rate Chinatown meals (from which wives and girlfriends are barred) that he shares greedily with a basically unglamorous, comfortable Gang of Four. The gang expands to include Puzo and Brooks and one or two others when they are in town, but more often consists of just Heller and three old buddies named George Mandel, Julius Green and "Speed" Vogel. Green is a successful small-business man, Vogel is a retired textile manufacturer and a former itinerant herring taster for Zabar's, and Mandel, who grew up with Heller in Coney Island, is a novelist and magazine writer.

Heller's social persona is most manifest in East Hampton, where he spends his summers. His one recent extravagance was the purchase of an expensive house there, not long after he began writing *Good as Gold*. It is a pleasant house, where he and his wife entertain at small, outdoor dinners, and it will soon have a swimming pool. But Heller does not look truly at ease in that setting.

"I've never known anyone so uncomfortable with fame," Puzo says. "We both became successes so late in life, we couldn't normalize ourselves. Writers like being alone. I visit Joe in East Hampton, but after a while I can sense he's dying to get rid of me."

Heller once confessed to his friend George Mandel, "I don't think I deserve all this money. It puts me into a class for which I have very little sympathy."

He has acquired no hobbies, sees few movies, attends the theater only occasionally (although he is devoted to good plays) and takes pleasure trips with misgiving and not much pleasure. What he most enjoys is reading, against a background of classical music. He is a lifelong, insatiable, retentive, analytical reader and it shows in his work. He skims off, here and there, what he needs to fuse with his own contorted attack. His comedy of despair is an unholy mutation, crossbred from [Franz] Kafka and [Fyodor] Dostoyevsky (Heller calls it "the literature of pain") with Lewis Carroll and Evelyn Waugh (the literature of malice and absurdity). At times he has tried (wistfully) for a dash of Oscar Wilde's elusive gloss, and (pensively) for a bit of O'Neillian thunder.

Heller Loves Food

Dwelling side by side with the intellectual connoisseur in Heller is the ravenous, undiscriminating gourmand. Food is inordinately important to him and it is difficult to be his friend if you don't enjoy eating. The characters in his novels do a lot of eating, some of it messy. When he describes a character in *Good as Gold* as being "unable to keep his hands off food, his own or others," he is talking about his own voracity at table. And he is expansive in analyzing the ingredients of a feast, prepared by members of Bruce Gold's family, that includes stuffed derma, noodle puddings, cheese blintzes, chopped liver, stuffed cabbage, chopped herring and matzoh balls. He has also described "Jewish corned-beef hash made with almost no potatoes and with hamburger meat and tomatoes rather than corned beef, which looked, even before the ketchup [was added] like a monstrous scarlet meat loaf."

Heller himself has to concentrate to control his weight. When he quit smoking in 1952, his weight shot up to well over 200 pounds. At 5 feet 11 1/2 inches (half an inch is curls), that was too much. Now he diets strenuously until dinner time. Outside the svelte Joe Heller is a fat person waiting to get back in. He has been known to eat two full meals at two separate restaurants in the course of one empty evening. He might eat three, if someone else were paying. (He doesn't realize he can afford to pay, or that he would be welcome practically anywhere, in spite of his unpredictable behavior.)

He was introduced to Craig Claiborne [food editor of *The New York Times*] one summer in East Hampton, where Claiborne lives year round. They hit it off and Claiborne invited Heller to dinner at his house, a sought-after privilege, fraught with the sort of social cachet Heller scorns. But he never scorns a free meal, even if it is *haute cuisine*; that is part of his pose. (Actually, he prefers large amounts of low cuisine.) The meal was an elaborate, cold buffet that Claiborne was writing up, and when Heller arrived, it was spread elegantly waiting to be photographed. The photographic equipment was set up, otherwise Heller would have been at the food instantly; as it was, he kept eyeing it, as he drank his Margaritas, circling ever closer, like a starved hound. The dining table was laid with pewter *sous assiettes* [underplates] that Heller, of course, mistook for the plates on which the guests would dine.

The instant the photographer removed his equipment, Heller seized a pewter underplate (the guests had not even been summoned to the table), piled it with mounds of everything, seated himself, and blissfully proceeded to empty his plate. Claiborne smiled indulgently. For some reason, he found Heller enchanting, and they have become friends, convinced that they share a maturity of outlook, and that they have, with age, achieved tranquillity. Claiborne will nod sagely as Heller tells him: "Thank goodness, we don't need love anymore. And without love, all we have left to worry about is passion, bliss and ecstasy." . . .

Essential Humor and Playfulness

Heller is a great appreciator of his own jokes, but he is also a generous laugher at the jokes of others. "He's the best laugher I know," says Mel Brooks. "He gives a lot back from a little joke. You need outfielders like that."

He has a sardonic laugh, a bitter laugh, a triumphant laugh, an apologetic laugh and a defensive laugh. As for his smile—described once by an unwary interviewer as "diffident"—it is about as diffident as that of the tiger from whose back the young lady from Niger mysteriously vanished. The smile is often pierced by a wooden, orange toothpick plucked from a packet Heller always carries. The toothpick appears immediately after a meal and sometimes lingers on into the night. Heller is no more couth than he is diffident.

One of his most striking characteristics is his accent. It is pure, unreconstructed, streets-of-New York (Noo Yawk). He also says "awff," "aloive," "toretchurred," "yumor" and "lidderacherr." And he stutters very slightly (a trait he gave to Slocum in *Something Happened*). The stutter is the way you know he is under stress—that, and a glazed look, accompanied by a laugh with a faintly nasty edge.

Heller has his serious moments. Mostly, they depress him. Ambivalent about practically everything, Heller, when he is working on a novel, hastens to the solitude of his studio and lunges at the day's work with a zest that soon wilts. Work never lasts more than two hours. He finds he cannot concentrate on his writing for longer than that.

"It's very hard, but interesting," he says, blandly. "I'm not a natural prose writer. I struggle to shape my sentences. I'm grateful to get any idea that will organize itself into a story. On the other hand, I've been able to use my repressions constructively, to very profitable effect, and to the entertainment and joy of millions.

As he dredges up bits of his life, Heller filters them *slowly* through his denial process before getting them down on paper, where he can make them belong, not to him, but to one of his protagonists.

"I know so many things I'm afraid to find out," says Slocum-Heller in *Something Happened.*

The line encompasses the essential Heller: his inverted humor, his cerebral playfulness, his psychologically sound intuition, the discernment to formulate a contradiction so true, the involuntary cringing of the man, and the compulsive exhibitionism of the author. . . .

Anxieties of the Creative Process

The idea for *Catch-22* came to Heller, as did the ideas for the two novels that followed, by a process he cannot precisely define, that he regards as a kind of magic, and that he does not care to question. "I get an opening line, and a concept of the book as a full, literary entity," he says. "It's all in my head before I even begin to write. Many of my ideas for dialogue and plot twists come to me while I'm jogging. And when I'm close to finishing a book, *nothing* is more important to me. I might stop to save a life, but nothing less." Heller pauses; the memory of his most recent period of fanaticism is still fresh.

"When my friend James Jones died, leaving his last novel incomplete, I began to be afraid *I* might die before finishing *Good as Gold*. Spookily, another friend, Robert Alan Aurthur, died last Nov. 20, leaving, like Jones, an unfinished project— the movie *All That Jazz* (he had collaborated on the script and was the producer). Aurthur admired Heller and occasionally admitted it; mostly the two needled each other with affection. Aurthur's wife, Jane, read me at my request a snippet of a diary entry left by her husband, dated [May 1978]. "Am to meet J.H. Both Joe and I agree book [*Good as Gold*] is a masterpiece. He wants to hear why I think so."

As Heller, for the third time, awaits publication of a new novel, he suffers from spells of anxiety (though pretending not to).

"I'll never write another book," he moans almost every time I talk to him. His muse is out of town. He broods, and gnaws on his nails.

Will the wrong reviewer like his novel for all the right reasons? Will the right reviewer like it for all the wrong reasons? Will copies be in the stores to coincide with his appearance on the *Today* show? Will he ever get another idea for a novel?

Should he go to Hollywood and write movies? Will anyone give him a job writing movies? Won't he ever get another idea for a novel?

He likes Los Angeles but would miss New York. New York has better hospitals for the care of the heart attack he will soon bring on from trying too hard to get an idea while jogging to stay in trim to avoid a heart attack. He would rather die laughing.

The Interplay of Comedy and Tragedy Characterize Heller's Life and Work

Judith Ruderman

Judith Ruderman is an academic administrator, professor, and author. She is vice provost for academic and administrative services at Duke University, where she also is an adjunct professor in the English department. Ruderman is also the author of several books and articles, including D.H. Lawrence and the Devouring Mother.

In the following article Judith Ruderman suggests that the revealing of a secret is central to each Heller work. She speculates that this could spring from two secrets that were withheld from the young Joseph Heller by his family for some time—his father's death at an early age and the fact that he and his siblings had different mothers. Also central to each Heller work, Ruderman argues, is his facing down his preoccupation with death through satire and irony.

Joseph Heller is a trickster. The pose he adopts in public is at times cynical, at times mischievous, on occasion frank. His novels disorient their readers, presenting surprises in technique, plot, and character. He enjoys playing practical jokes in real life as well, and his sense of humor is often so dry that one cannot be sure if he is serious or not, or even happy or sad. A rapid interplay and confusion between tragedy and comedy characterizes both the life and the art, so that in a sense Heller has been the central character in a Jewish joke, and his story exemplifies that Jewish humor he defines, in *Good as Gold*, as the ironic, fatalistic mockery of the Talmud and the shtetl [Jewish neighborhood].

Judith Ruderman, "Angst for the Memories: The Life and Times of Joseph Heller," in *Joseph Heller*, Danvers, MA: Continuum Publishing Co., 1991, pp. 15–29. Copyright © 1991 by Judith Ruderman. Reproduced by permission of the author.

Secrets Central to Heller's Life and Fiction

Born in the New York City borough of Brooklyn on May 1, 1923, Heller was brought up in what he has called "moderate poverty" in a "depressed" residential neighborhood of Coney Island, located on Brooklyn's southern rim. Nearly all the Coney Islanders of his parents' generation were immigrants from Eastern Europe. His mother, Lena, about thirty-eight years of age at his birth, spoke little English; his father, Isaac, roughly the same age as his wife, had emigrated from Russia a decade earlier and earned his living in this country as a bakery truck driver. Isaac Heller suffered from ulcers that his wife attributed to the quantities of bakery cake he consumed. When Joseph was four, in 1927, his father died after an ulcer operation that went wrong. The mother never remarried, and Heller began to think of his brother, Lee—who was fourteen years older and born in Russia—as his father. At the age of eight or nine, in fact, he gave Lee a Father's Day gift with the note, "You're like a father to me." Not until Lee's wedding, when Heller was fifteen, did he discover that both Lee and Sylvia, his sister, had had a different mother than he, a not uncommon occurrence in immigrant families. This "secret" was the second one to astound and infuriate the boy. Upon his father's death, he was not told what had happened but rather was left to wonder why there were so many people and so much food in the house that day. Perhaps it is no coincidence, then, that secrets—their concealing and their revealing—are at the heart of every Heller book. . . .

Early Work Is Formulaic

Heller composed his earliest story, about the Russian invasion of Finland, at ten or eleven years of age, on a neighbor boy's typewriter. He offered it to the *Daily News*, which published one short story a day, but the piece was rejected. Undaunted, he continued writing and submitting fiction to various periodicals, with no luck. His best subject at Abraham Lincoln High School was English Composition. After graduation in

1941 he clerked in the file room of a casualty insurance company, and then, after Pearl Harbor, worked as a blacksmith's helper for a short time at the Norfolk Navy Yard. In 1942, at nineteen, he enlisted in the Army Air Corps and spent three years in service, one of them (1944–45) in combat on Corsica with the 488th squadron, 340th Bombardment Group, 12th Air Force. After short service as a public relations officer in San Angelo, Texas, Heller was discharged from the air force as a first lieutenant, with an Air Medal and a Presidential Unit Citation.

Heller had been anxious for combat. Propagandistic war movies and a firm belief in the righteousness of the cause made warfare appear "dramatic and heroic" to this young soldier. In fact, he flew sixty combat missions in a B-25 over Italy and France; but on the thirty-seventh mission, over Avignon, he thought his plane had exploded and consequently was terrified on all his remaining flights. He vowed that if he lived through the war he would avoid airplanes entirely and, at war's end, took a ship back home to the States to prove his point (though he changed his mind about flying in 1960, after enduring a twenty-four-hour train trip from New York to Miami). While overseas Heller kept a diary of his missions, and he also composed short fiction. When stationed in Texas he submitted two of these pieces to *Story* magazine, edited by Whit Burnett. Burnett accepted one—"I Don't Love You Anymore"—for a servicemen's issue in the fall of 1945, when Heller was twenty-two. An account not of this serviceman's martial adventures, but rather of a marital spat in which the husband refuses to put on clothes to greet his company, Heller's first published work was later called by its own author "decidedly inferior." The year 1945 also marked Heller's marriage to Brooklyn native Shirley Held, whom he had met on a weekend furlough at a Catskill Mountains resort. Their two children are Erica, now in her late thirties, and Ted, four years younger, both of them graduates, like their father, of New York University, with interests in writing and film.

After the war, Heller enrolled briefly at the University of Southern California under the GI Bill before transferring, with Whit Burnett's help, to New York University. As a sophomore, at age twenty-three or so, he took a creative writing course with Maurice Baudin, a specialist in seventeenth- and eighteenth-century French drama. He submitted for publication the stories that Baudin praised and sold two of them to *Esquire* and two to the *Atlantic Monthly*. One of these—"Castle of Snow"—was included in *The Best Short Stories of 1949*. Deciding he liked the two hundred dollars that the *Atlantic* paid him, he tried for $1,500 from *Good Housekeeping*, but his hack work did not meet with success. Heller was writing a good deal of serious fiction at this time, the mid-1940s, and has characterized his work as "*New Yorker* type stories, by Jewish writers about Jewish life in Brooklyn." Heller's assessment of his early stories does not apply to the ones that saw print: of his publications between 1945 and 1948, only "Castle of Snow" is clearly on the subject of Jews. Reminiscent of Hemingway, especially in their heavy reliance on dialogue, these stories are, on the whole, formulaic (to use [critic] David Seed's word for them); they conform to the type of fiction then being published in such magazines as the *Atlantic, Collier's, Esquire*, and *The New Yorker*, in which a gradual release of information reveals the true subject underneath the surface. Though derivative, these stories obviously contained a spark of something highly original, for by his senior year in college, Heller was already considered one of the country's most promising young writers. And, it should be noted here, the gradual release of information would remain a Heller trademark throughout his career as a novelist.

Begins Work on a War Novel

After graduating Phi Beta Kappa from NYU in 1948, Heller took a master's in American literature from Columbia University with a thesis entitled "The Pulitzer Prize Plays: 1917–1935." He then studied English literature—especially Chaucer, Shakespeare, and Milton—at St. Catherine's College, Oxford

University, for a year as a Fulbright Scholar, though he seems to have spent a good portion of his time working on a short story. His first job was teaching freshman composition at Pennsylvania State College (now University) for several semesters, but in 1952 he left State College and academics for the more congenial territory of New York's advertising world. For a decade he worked in the "copy and promo" business at *Time* (1952–56), *Look* (1956–58), and *McCall's* (1958–61) magazines, as well as at Remington Rand. As a copywriter at *Time* in 1955, Heller prepared texts for slide shows to assist the advertising-space salesmen in securing business for the magazine. He also worked on his first novel, for which he had begun making notes a couple of years earlier, while at Remington Rand. In fact, the archives of *Story* magazine reveal that Heller was planning a war novel as early as 1945, and that Whit Burnett read four chapters of this work not long afterward. Correspondence between Burnett and Heller suggests that the novel in this form was rather conventional, and that Burnett's advice and encouragement were instrumental in Heller's eventual choice of creative writing as a career. At any rate, Heller had abandoned this novel and the fresh start was apparently leading in a different direction. Although the novel in progress in the mid-fifties was set in World War II, times had changed in the years since D-Day. A new conflict was raging in Korea and the cold war was now a reality. The unified American opinion on war had disintegrated, and the country was shaken and divided over issues ranging from civil rights to nuclear armaments. The main aspect of Heller's new "war novel" true to the war as he had experienced it was the fear of dying in combat. Otherwise the work does not stand up as a realistic or even interesting record of World War II. Rather, as Heller notes, he "deliberately seeded the book with anachronisms like loyalty oaths, helicopters, IBM machines and agricultural subsidies to create the feeling of American society from the McCarthy period on."

The opening line of the novel, then called *Catch-18* rather than *Catch-22*, came to Heller as he was lying in bed one night in 1955 and thinking of author Louis-Ferdinand Céline. Céline's *Journey to the End of the Night* (1932) may be said to have ignited Heller, for "Céline did things with time and structure and colloquial speech I'd never experienced before." In that year Heller wrote, rewrote, and published his first chapter, "The Texan," in *New World Writing no. 7*, a quarterly anthology devoted to sections of books in progress. In 1957, Heller's agent sent some 250 pages of the novel to Simon and Schuster, where they were read over a several-month period by a young editorial assistant named Robert Gottlieb (who went on to be president of Alfred A. Knopf and now edits the *New Yorker* magazine). Gottlieb reports that he "didn't know enough" to be wary of such provocative, innovative writing—"I just figured if something were that good, it would eventually become a success," he recounts—and offered Heller a contract to publish, with a $1,500 advance: half on signing and half on acceptance of the manuscript. Heller continued to write his novel in the evenings after work, two or three hours a night, for seven or eight years altogether. "I gave up once and started watching television with my wife," he recalls. "Television drove me back to *Catch-22*. I couldn't imagine what Americans did at night when they weren't writing novels." The flip side to Heller's flippant remark is found in other comments that expose his frustration at the tedious process of eking out a first novel word by precious word, one page a night: "It came so hard I really thought it would be the only thing I ever wrote," he has admitted.

Catch-22 Is Published

Work continued on this novel when Heller hired on as a copywriter in the marketing division at *Look* in 1960. Uninterested in the business of preparing sales presentations based on numbers or analysis, he poured his energies into his book, on which he often worked behind closed doors with his boss's tacit permission. Finally, when Heller was thirty-eight years old and by then a promotion manager at *McCall's, Catch-18* was completed. Since Leon Uris had recently published a novel *Mila 18*, Gottlieb came up with the idea of changing Heller's title to *Catch-22* in order to avoid confusion. Both author and editor liked the repetition of number in the new title since it was appropriate to the repetition in the novel itself. *Catch-22*, much reduced in size from Heller's eight-hundred-page manuscript, was published by Simon and Schuster in September 1961. Its mixed reception is well exemplified by the *New York Times*, which one day described the novel as "gasping for want of craft and sensibility" and the next as "a dazzling performance." In fact, the publication might have caused no stir at all except that S.J. Perelman, in an interview in the *New York Herald Tribune*, mentioned that he had just read a good new book, by Joseph Heller. *Catch-22* never sold enough copies in a single week to appear on the *Times*'s best-seller list, and Heller has said that the novel fulfilled all his fantasies save two: it didn't make him rich and it wasn't on that all-important list. But it did sell thirty-two thousand copies in the first year, and when the paperback came out from Dell in October 1962 it was an immediate hit, with over two million copies sold in one year. Indeed, *Catch-22* has been called "the American counter-culture bible of the 1960's."

Heller Becomes a Screenwriter

The year 1962 was a good one for Heller. Columbia pictures bought the movie rights to *Catch-22*, enabling Heller to leave his advertising job at *McCall's*. He was hired to write the screenplay, but waived his right to do so. . . . During the mid-sixties Heller taught creative writing classes in fiction and drama at the University of Pennsylvania one day a week and at Yale another. In the early 1950s Heller had collaborated on a movie script for Twentieth Century-Fox with a colleague at

Penn State College. Described as a spy spoof, "The Trieste Manuscripts" was never produced but it did prepare the way for further work on comedy scripts in the 1960s. These ventures, undertaken solely for money, resulted in several imbroglios of one degree or another. Hired in 1962 to write a pilot script to launch "McHale's Navy," a television series, Heller got involved in a seven-year legal dispute over revisions made without his consent. He went to Hollywood to collaborate on *Sex and the Single Girl*, released in 1964, and found that the $5,000 a week he received did not quite overcome his dislike of the movie colony's cavalier attitude toward words. After doctoring a number of scenes in the James Bond spoof *Casino Royale* (1967), Heller discovered that several other writers (including Woody Allen) had been working on the script as well. Out of this experience Heller created his own spoof, a comic fiction called "How I Found James Bond, Lost My Self-Respect, and Almost Made $150,000 in My Spare Time," published in *Holiday* magazine in 1967. In style and subject matter this story echoes *Catch-22*, with the director as the "heavy" and finishing the script itself as slippery, a mission as completing the requisite number of bombing raids.

No battle scars seem to have been received from Heller's other screen adaptations of the period, his work on his friend George Mandel's novel *The Breakwater* (1960) and his collaboration with Tom and Frank Waldman on *Dirty Dingus Magee* (1970). (Heller was also invited to work on *Doctor Strangelove*, an antiwar send-up of military armament very much in keeping with the tone of *Catch-22*.) But his financial dealings over the movie rights to *Catch-22* again led to a comical commentary, this time on his agent Irving Lazar. Though complimentary of Lazar's accomplishments, the sketch—"Irving Is Everywhere," published in *Show* magazine in 1963—implicitly faults his values (with good reason David Seed draws a comparison to *Catch-22's* Milo Minderbinder). Although Heller had a mixed reaction to the film version of his first novel, the movie was in fact very good for his career. In mid-1970, with the appearance of Mike Nichols's film version, created from a screenplay by Buck Henry, the novel set a record for paperback sales during one six-week period, though the film itself lost fifteen million dollars and was the financial disaster of the year. (One cannot help noting the Helleresque fact that the pretend martial armaments in the movie constituted the world's twelfth largest bomber force at the time!) The term *catch-22* is now firmly embedded in *Webster's* between *catchpole* and *catchup* and the novel *Catch-22* is firmly entrenched in the modern literary canon, required reading even at the US Air Force Academy, which hosted a scholarly symposium in 1986 to commemorate the novel's twenty-fifth anniversary. One hears the phrase regularly, in the House of Representatives and on the street. American soldiers in Vietnam are said to have carried copies of the novel in their backpacks. By 1988 the work had sold more than twenty-five million copies and its popularity shows no sign of abating. College students, especially, love it.

In the 1960s Heller also toured the country in opposition to the Vietnam War, and was so disgusted with politics that he did not vote for president until George McGovern was the candidate in 1972; indeed, he ran as an anti-Johnson delegate (favoring Eugene McCarthy) in the 1968 presidential primary. He also voted for Senator Keating in New York against Bobby Kennedy because Keating spoke out against American involvement in Vietnam. Heller is so disillusioned with the political process that he has not voted in an election in almost two decades. . . .

Guillain-Barré Syndrome

In December of 1981 [Heller] began feeling weak and having some difficulty swallowing, but his minor complaints were ignored by his friends because Heller had always been known as something of a hypochondriac. Only when Heller became unable to remove his sweater, cross his right leg over his left, open his jaws wide enough to tackle a tuna-fish sandwich, or perform a number of other hitherto routine tasks did he realize that something was seriously wrong with him. His doctors' immediate diagnosis was Guillain-Barré, called a syndrome rather than a disease because only its aggregate symptoms and the course they take can verify its existence. It is an illness experienced by a small number of people—fewer than two Americans out of every one hundred thousand come down with it each year—and its severity is different, unpredictably so, in each case. Heller's physicians could not know at the beginning whether he would survive, and whether he would regain his faculties 100 percent if he did so. They could only hope to keep him alive until his body of its own accord stopped producing antibodies that were destroying the myelin sheathes around his nerve fibers.

In *Catch-22*, the goldbricking Yossarian tells Milo Minderbinder that he has Garnett-Fleischaker syndrome, and that "a good Garnett-Fleischaker syndrome isn't easy to come by." Heller's Guillain-Barré wasn't easy to come by either, given the odds against it, especially if one did not have the swine flu shot that was associated with it in the seventies. To quote another wag, Heller's friend Mario Puzo, "When they name any disease after two guys, it's got to be terrible!" Unlike Yossarian—who, after all, was only kidding about his syndrome—Heller was terribly ill for many months. Unable to swallow, he was fed by a tube in his nose and had secretions cleared from his mouth by a suction tube. His speech was slurred, his breath short. By the fifth day after his admission to the hospital he could not sit up. And gradually he got worse. With tubes in his orifices and patients dying around him, Heller must have felt something like his own soldier in white from *Catch-22*, lacking only the mummylike bindings and the garrulous Texan (though he did have Mel Brooks to drive him to distraction with conversation). Certainly his friends noticed the resemblance to Heller's fictional character.

Within a short period of time—just a couple of weeks—Heller deteriorated physically as much as he was going to; but, though his Guillain-Barré was stable, he was increasingly depressed about his condition and the prospects of a prolonged hospital stay. Heller saw a psychiatrist regularly and, with his saving sense of humor, "found him useful even when discussing such trivial problems as the Oedipal complex, repetition compulsions, the impact on children of the death of parents, and the character and psychology" of some of the specialists on the case. Soon he began to improve, and after three weeks in intensive care he was moved into a private room. One of his new nurses was Valerie Humphries, who understood his muffled speech, laughed at his jokes, and liked food as much as he did—a winning combination of attributes. Three weeks later, Nurse Humphries moved over to the Rusk Institute when her patient was transferred there for rehabilitation. . . .

After a courtship of some four years, Heller married Valerie Humphries in April 1987, Yossarian never had it so good with Nurse Duckett.

No Laughing Matter

An article written by Speed Vogel for the *New York Times* about "Helping a Convalescent Friend (in Style)," and a subsequent interview with Heller in *People* magazine, resulted in a flood of letters to East Hampton and a surge of interest in Heller's bout with Guillain-Barré. Vogel began to consider writing a book about his experiences with his friend's illness, to be called *Poor Speed, His Friend Joe Is Sick*, but the friend himself got into the act as coauthor. According to Heller, *No Laughing Matter*, published by G.P. Putnam's Sons in February 1986, with alternating chapters by Heller and Vogel, is not a "medical book" but "more a story about friendship." It is also a story about divorce, and a means for letting off some steam at lawyers. Although readers curious about, or touched in some way by, Guillain-Barré syndrome will find much in the book to hold their attention, *No Laughing Matter* is of greatest merit to the Heller aficionado because, in lieu of a biography or autobiography, it is the most sustained portrait to date (other than his novels) of the man's personality and relationships. The interplay among Heller's cronies—the wisecracking, the horseplay, the insults, the affection—is as entertaining as any borscht belt routine . . . as any Heller novel, for that matter. And, like the humor in Heller's novels, it is a way of holding despair at arm's length. The alternating chapters set up intriguing contrasts in perspective (Heller's catastrophe is Vogel's meal ticket) and also highlight the ironical approach to an important subtext: death. Speed Vogel's concluding section, which depicts in sentimental terms the demise of Joseph Heller, is counterpointed by Heller's vigorous denial of that ending. As David Seed cogently analyzes this section of *No Laughing Matter*, "The serious point behind this textual joking is that the possibility that Heller might die (in the background throughout the first part of the book) is now made explicit as comic fiction which simultaneously confronts the possibility and drains it of serious threat."

Speed Vogel would have us believe that Heller's personality underwent a sea change in combat with that mild case of Guillain-Barré. He reports, "Before Heller's big affliction, his close and dear friends used to commiserate with each other about his exceptional impatience, rudeness, insensitivity, selfishness, arrogance, duplicity, obstinacy, malevolence, insincerity, negativity, and general unpleasantness. We liked him . . . but we were extremely hard put to explain why." Afterwards, in Vogel's view, Heller became a nice guy. Heller himself reports that life became uncomplicated and uncluttered when he retired to East Hampton to get better: "My problems were few and I knew what they were." One tends to doubt that this *harmonious* side to Heller has survived his convalescence, at least not intact. And one almost hopes that it has not. . . .

Sequel to *Catch-22*

Joseph Heller is now approaching threescore and ten [in 1991]. He has taken his own (bitter)sweet time to write his five novels to date, but his major works of fiction are coming with increasing speed the older he gets. After a lifetime of hypochondria and compulsive jogging and dieting—"I'm preoccupied with death, disease, and misfortune," Heller said in 1973—he has conquered illness and debilitation and is writing energetically in East Hampton. He plans not only the sequel to *Catch-22* but also another nonfiction collaboration with Speed Vogel, this one about their contrasting childhoods in New York. Unlike his King David, Heller is not a lonely old man looking back on his deathbed over a life filled with disappointments, fearful of dying yet sick of living. He says that he is in "the twilight of [his] career," yet perhaps now, more than ever, he would echo the sentiments voiced to an interviewer over a decade ago: "I've come to look upon death the same way I look upon root canal work. Everyone else seems to get through it all right, so it couldn't be too difficult for me."

Catch-22 Was a Groundbreaking Novel of the 1960s

Stephen W. Potts

Stephen W. Potts is a professor and writer. He teaches in the Department of Literature at the University of California at San Diego and is the author of several books and articles on contemporary authors. He is also the creator of Armageddon Buffet, *an online journal of fiction and commentary.*

In the following selection, Stephen W. Potts finds that by the end of the 1950s and the Eisenhower era, American critics were seeking a change from the realistic novel. Heller was the first of several authors to strike out in a bold new direction with Catch-22, *a work that combined the satirical and surreal. Potts considers* Catch-22 *to be a representative work of the socially and politically chaotic sixties, as well as the best novel of the decade.*

By the end of the decade of the fifties, with its smug, even soporific conservatism, American intellectual culture was restless. Historian Arthur Schlesinger, Jr., expressed the discontent of his fellow intellectuals in an article in the January 1960 *Esquire*. After insisting that a new desire for change was rumbling beneath the "passivity and acquiescence" of the Eisenhower epoch, he goes on to say:

> As yet, the feeling is inchoate and elusive. But it is beginning to manifest itself in a multitude of ways: in freshening attitudes in politics; in a new acerbity in criticism; in stirrings, often tinged with desperation, among the youth; in a spread-

Stephen W. Potts, "The Importance of the Work," in *Catch 22: Antiheroic Antinovel*, Twayne Masterwork Studies, no. 29, Belmont, CA: Twayne Publishers, 1989, pp. 5–8. Copyright © 1989 by G.K. Hall & Company. All rights reserved. Reproduced by permission of Gale, a part of Cengage Learning.

ing contempt everywhere for reigning clichés. There is evident a widening restlessness, dangerous tendencies toward satire and idealism, a mounting dissatisfaction with the official priorities, a deepening concern with our character and objectives as a nation.

The 1960s Ushered in a New Culture

Among the examples he gives of this cultural foment are the rise of the Beats, the sudden efflorescence of satire and "sick humor," and the popularity of books critical of American culture and capitalism, such as [John Kenneth] Galbraith's *The Affluent Society*, [David] Riesman's *The Lonely Crowd*, and [William] Whyte's *The Organization Man*.

In American literary circles many critics were seeking an alternative for the mainstream mimetic novel [a novel that mimics reality], which had been pronounced dead by a number of them following the great prewar era that had produced the masterpieces of the modernist canon. For many, James Joyce's *Ulysses* and *Finnegans Wake* had taken the realistic novel as far as it could go, even to the brink of mythic fantasy. Many looked for guidance to Europe, and France in particular, where they found the existentialist novels of [Albert] Camus and [Jean-Paul] Sartre, the Theater of the Absurd, and the *nouvelle roman* [new novel] of Alain Robbe-Grillet. None translated well to the needs of American fiction, however.

Other possibilities were suggested by the fiction of Vladimir Nabokov and Argentinian Jorge Luis Borges. As later noted by English critic Tony Tanner in his 1971 study *City of Words*, Nabokov and Borges took up the challenge left by Joyce. Both had begun in the realistic tradition that the twentieth century inherited from the nineteenth, but steered into newer realms of invention with the examples of Joyce and [Franz] Kafka in their back pockets. Both authors offered the further advantage, for Americans, of being alienated from their own cultures and thus cosmopolitan in outlook— Nabokov was the scion of an aristocratic Russian family transplanted to central Europe and then America, Borges received the whole of his education in Europe—and for both English was a second language. Both had caught the attention of the American literary intelligentsia in the 1950s, Borges with his collection *Fictions*, Nabokov with *Lolita*: both works had been first published and celebrated in France.

Amid the literary ferment of letters after Joyce, amid the restlessness and satire and general questioning of American political and artistic values, the new decade of the sixties began. Arthur Schlesinger, Jr., predicted that it would be "spirited, articulate, inventive, incoherent, turbulent, with energy shooting off wildly in all directions."

Into this environment in the first year of the [John F.] Kennedy presidency came *Catch-22*. As the blurb inside the book jacket of the first hardcover edition notes, "CATCH-22 is like no other novel we have ever read. It has its own style, its own rationale, its own extraordinary character. It moves back and forth from hilarity to horror. It is outrageously funny and strangely affecting. It is totally original." Many reviewers agreed. They recognized the novel's links with war humor and black humor, but the blend of farce, fierce violence, sharp satire, and the avant-garde method of the plot set *Catch-22* apart.

The First Postmodern Novel

In fact, *Catch-22* was the first of a slew of novels in the early sixties that represented a new direction in American literature, combining naturalistic detail with satirical and surreal exaggeration, mingling slapstick and gloom, fantasy and history, real issues and two-dimensional caricatures that are at best reminiscent of Charles Dickens. Other works of this groundbreaking moment are Ken Kesey's *One Flew Over the Cuckoo's Nest* (1962), Kurt Vonnegut's *Mother Night* (1961) and *Cat's Cradle* (1963), and Thomas Pynchon's *V* (1963). Not until the 1970s would American critics recognize that these novels were not aberrations fitting loosely within the black humor genre,

An illustration of a "Catch-22"—a machine shaking the hand of a man with one of its arms and preparing to punch him in the back as he does so. © Images.com/Corbis.

but the advance guard of a whole new approach to the novel, a movement now generally given the term "postmodernism."

But postmodernism was not even a glimmer in the critic's eye when *Catch-22* reached the British best-seller lists in its first year. And the novel's American readership was probably hooked as much on the book's message as on its method. In this Heller was helped along by national events. By the middle of the decade the "police action" in Vietnam was heating up to a full-scale war under President [Lyndon B.] Johnson and both progressive intellectuals and college students began to show an increasing annoyance with the liberal regime that had come in with the late JFK. By 1965 Berkeley's Free Speech movement had caught the attention of other campus activists, and increasingly the idealism that had earlier been channeled into civil rights and the Peace Corps began to mobilize against the growing war and America's cold war foreign policy in general, and from there against every aspect of American life as represented by "the Establishment."

Where the more sullen, quietly rebellious college students of the 1950s had embraced J.D. Salinger and Jack Kerouac, the activist readers of the 1960s—having graduated from the satirical if sophomoric sick humor of *Mad* magazine to the sterner leftist critiques of [philosopher] Herbert Marcuse and [sociologist] Paul Goodman—found their confirmation in the pointed social satires of Heller, Vonnegut, and Kesey. Of all the innovative books of radical style and social criticism, *Catch-22* is probably the most encyclopedic in the number of issues it touches on; in so completely capturing the frustration of the individual up against powerful and faceless bureaucracies, it gave the American language a new term in "Catch-22," which has come to refer to any situation encompassing paradoxical choices, usually imposed from above.

Identified with the Antiwar Movement

Heller could honestly claim that his novel was not intended as a criticism of World War II, or initially even of war in general; that its satire was aimed at the cold war of the fifties is clear, he observed in interviews, from the pointed use of anachronisms such as loyalty oaths, helicopters, and IBM machines. Nonetheless, in the eyes of the youth of the time Heller and

his novel were most identified with the antiwar issue, an iden-
tification he encouraged with his 1969 antiwar play *We
Bombed in New Haven*. When, at the end of the decade, the
novel was filmed by Mike Nichols (long a satirist in his own
right), it joined a string of darkly humorous antiwar films
with a youthful cult following: *Dr. Strangelove, How I Won the
War* (featuring John Lennon), and *M*A*S*H*.

With the coming of the seventies campus activism faded
away, as eventually, and ignominiously, did the war itself and
the presidents who conducted it. But as *Catch-22* moved from
backpack to assigned reading list the stature of the novel remained secure. As one of the first and most original creations
of literary postmodernism and as an artifact of the social and
political culture of the sixties, it is still regarded by many as
the best novel of the decade.

| *Catch-22* and War

Catch-22 Is the Best American Novel in Many Years

Nelson Algren

Nelson Algren was an author, journalist, essayist, critic, and teacher of creative writing. His best-known work of fiction is the National Book Award–winning The Man with the Golden Arm.

When Catch-22 *was first published, it was unlike any novel critics had seen, and, as a result, most reviews were mixed or unfavorable. A notable exception was this important review by award-winning author Nelson Algren, who described* Catch-22 *as not only superior to such classic World War II novels as Norman Mailer's* The Naked and the Dead *and James Jones's* From Here to Eternity, *but also as one of the best American novels in years.*

There was only one catch and that was Catch-22, which specified that a concern for one's own safety in the face of dangers that were real and immediate was the process of a rational mind. Orr was crazy and could be grounded. All he had to do was ask; and as soon as he did, he would no longer be crazy and would have to fly more missions. He would be crazy to fly more missions and sane if he didn't, but if he was sane he had to fly them. Yossarian was moved very deeply by the absolute simplicity of this clause and let out a respectful whistle:

"That's some catch, that Catch-22," he observed.

"It's the best there is," Doc Daneeka agreed.

Yossarian was moved deeply day and night and what moved him more deeply than anything else was the fact that they were trying to murder him.

Nelson Algren, "The Catch," *The Nation*, vol. 193, November 4, 1961, p. 358. Copyright © 1961 by The Nation Magazine/The Nation Company, Inc. Copyright renewed 1989 by The Nation Co. Reproduced by permission.

"Who's 'they'?" Clevenger wanted to know. "Who, specifically, is trying to murder you?"

"Every one of them," Yossarian told him.

"Every one of whom?"

"Every one of whom do you think?"

"I haven't any idea."

"Then how do you know they aren't?"

Yossarian had proof, because strangers he didn't know shot at him with cannons every time he flew up into the air to drop bombs on them, so it was of no use for Clevenger to say "No one is trying to kill you."

"Then why are they shooting at me?"

"They're shooting at everyone."

"And what difference does that make?"

"I'm not going to argue with you," Clevenger decided, "you don't know who you hate."

"Whoever is trying to poison me."

"Nobody is trying to poison you."

"They poisoned my food twice, didn't they? Didn't they put poison in my food at Ferrara and during the Great Big Siege of Bologna?"

"They put poison in everybody's food," Clevenger explained.

"And what difference does that make?"

There was no established procedure for evasive action. All you needed was fear, and Yossarian had plenty of that. He bolted wildly for his life on each mission the instant his bombs were away. When he fulfilled the thirty-five missions required of each man of his group, he asked to be sent home.

Colonel Cathcart had by then raised the missions required to forty. When Yossarian had flown forty he asked to be sent home. Colonel Cathcart had raised the missions required to forty-five—there did seem to be a catch somewhere. Yossarian went into the hospital with a pain in his liver that fell just short of being jaundice. If it became jaundice the doctors could treat it. If it didn't become jaundice and went away they could discharge him. Yossarian decided to spend the rest of the war in bed by running a daily temperature of 101. He had found a catch of his own.

To preserve his sanity against the formalized lunacy of the military mind in action, Yossarian had to turn madman. Yet even Yossarian is more the patriot than Sgt. Minderbinder, the business mind in action. Even Yossarian has to protest when Minderbinder arranges with the Germans to let them knock American planes down at a thousand dollars per plane. Minderbinder is horrified—"Have you no respect for the sanctity of a business contract?" he demands of Yossarian, and Yossarian feels ashamed of himself.

Beneath the Humor Is Horror

Below its hilarity, so wild that it hurts, *Catch-22* is the strongest repudiation of our civilization, in fiction, to come out of World War II. *The Naked and the Dead* [by Norman Mailer] and *From Here to Eternity* [by James Jones] are lost within it. That the horror and the hypocrisy, the greed and the complacency, the endless cunning and the endless stupidity which now go to constitute what we term Christianity are dealt with here in absolutes, does not lessen the truth of its repudiation. Those happy few who hit upon Terry Southern's *The Magic Christian* will find that, what Southern said with some self-doubt, Heller says with no doubt whatsoever. To compare *Catch-22* favorably with *The Good Soldier Schweik* [by Jaroslav

Hašek] would be an injustice, because this novel is not merely the best American novel to come out of World War II; it is the best American novel that has come out of anywhere in years.

Heller Combines Realism with Surrealism to Create a New Genre: the Neo-Satiric War Novel

Jeffrey Walsh

Jeffrey Walsh is an author, editor, and professor who taught at Manchester Metropolitan University in England. He is the author or editor of several works on modern warfare, including The Gulf War Did Not Happen: Politics, Culture and Warfare Post-Vietnam.

In the following selection, Jeffrey Walsh contends that Joseph Heller established the labyrinth as a symbol of war in Catch-22 *in the same way that the lingering impact of fighting had symbolized World War I. The catch-22 of the title acts metaphorically in several ways to reinforce the helplessness of the soldiers in the face of the bureaucracy of the military-industrial complex. Heller is unique as a novelist, Walsh contends, for the way in which he infuses traditional elements of the war novel with neo-satiric elements, thus forging a new genre.*

Catch-22 (1961) has probably contributed more than any other work to the literary apprehension of war during the last two decades. The interpenetration between literary form and the movements of history is clearly shown in the commercial success of Heller's labyrinthine novel: the symbolisation of war as a labyrinth has now become firmly established in the way that earlier myths had been (the First World War metaphor of the soldier's farewell to arms was a previous example of equally potent symbolism); such images act as pri-

Jeffrey Walsh, "Towards Vietnam: Portraying Modern War," in *American War Literature: 1914 to Vietnam*, New York: St. Martin's Press, 1982, pp. 185–207. Copyright © Jeffrey Walsh 1982. Reproduced by permission of the author.

mary vehicles for our consciousness of men at arms. It is hardly an exaggeration to say that the idea of an all-pervasive catch has become the most widely accepted image of battle Pentagon-style, its structures and forms. Heller's invention of a catch which simultaneously determines, reflects and distorts the attitudes of various ranks of soldiers to the deadness of military institutionalism symbolises most effectively the nature of hegemonic relations. The intellectual genesis of the catch is difficult to identify, although one can take pleasure in drawing analogies with the processes of formal logic or such complex constructs as those inspired by generative grammar. The catch, of course, coerces, yet in a barely perceived manner which relies upon intellectual beauty and coherence:

> Yossarian saw it clearly in all its spinning reasonableness. There was an elliptical precision about its perfect pairs of parts that was graceful and shocking, like good modern art, and at times Yossarian wasn't quite sure that he saw it at all, just the way he was never quite sure about good modern art.

Catch Works on Several Levels

The catch obliquely implies the reification of military procedures in its formal autonomy; its uses, as the novel reveals, are exploitative. Through its mystique and *Gestalt*-like powers[1] the catch may be drawn upon in a variety of ways to instil loyalty and obedience to the military creed. It may provide legitimation for raising the number of bombing missions or justify the arrest of persons thought to be opposed to the bureaucratic hierarchy. The metaphor of a catch works structurally and imaginatively to symbolise in microcosm the seemingly willing mass subjection of soldiers to the interests of the industrial-military complex. Colonel Korn's educational sessions supply an example of the infallible theory in operation:

1. The term *Gestalt* denotes experiences that require more than basic sensory capacities to comprehend; the perception of intangible background context.

only men who never ask questions are admitted, and then the sessions are discontinued on the grounds that it was neither possible nor necessary to educate people who never questioned anything.

Taken at this level *Catch-22* embodies a satire upon system building, a hypostastisation directed at grammarians, logicians and positivists in a neo-Swiftian mode. [Critic] Tony Tanner has drawn attention to the abiding concern of American writers with conspiracy theories, their fear that the simple 'unpatterned' life, inward-directed (and analogous with the mythical past of the virginal continent) becomes impossible to achieve in a world where individual identity is increasingly obfuscated (as the extended word-play upon the names of characters in Heller's masterpiece suggests); spontaneous conduct grows more and more difficult. Tanner emphasises the role of behaviourism and the linguistic sciences in convincing Americans that freedom of action is more and more constricted:

> American writers dread . . . all conditioning forces to the point of paranoia which is detectable not only in the subject matter of many novels but also in their narrative devices. Narrative lines are full of hidden persuaders, hidden dimensions, plots, secret organisation, evil systems, all kinds of conspiracies against spontaneity of consciousness, even cosmic take over. The possible nightmare of being totally controlled by unseen agencies and powers is never far away in contemporary American fiction. The unease revealed in such novels is related to a worried apprehension on the part of the author that his own consciousness may be predetermined and channelled by the language he has been born into.

Given that the long tradition (from [Spanish philosopher José] Ortega Y Gasset to [American philosopher Herbert] Marcuse) of predicting the growth of dehumanisation has authentic roots, the artist is increasingly likely to create literary modes which permit him to portray a social world of an indeterminate and anxious character, and one inimical to the individual's rational understanding. Heller's fictional work displays these features, and his formal procedures such as the devices of satiric distortion, allegory, parody and burlesque contribute to the formation of a vision of breakdown. His novel exploits the departure from literal truth in order to arrive at a representation of the monolithic power of modern institutions, in this case conveyed through the metaphor of the army's hierarchy. Such bewilderment experienced by the reader throughout the novel seems warranted if *Catch-22* is read in this way as a new kind of satire, one whose elaborate fabrications communicate a profound national *Angst*. One example should make this clear, the way individual generals are as helpless as their men, which is shown in their over-sensitivity to the media; their wish to be presented in a favourable light indicates that they are as much victims of 'the system' as the combat airmen trying to escape from flying more bombing missions. The image communicated throughout the novel is of men lost in psychological corridors.

Catch-22 Reflects Its Era

If one accepts such an interpretation of the novel, *Catch-22* exhibits certain characteristics of its period. The novel, for example, bases its narrative upon a fluctuating rhythm of crisis. One may observe a parallel development in the public's response to war as conveyed through the media and newspapers: many of the latter reserve a section of their foreign news pages for the coverage of wars abroad, and the most acclaimed newspaper men tend to be those frequently prominent in front-line action. Another obvious relation of Heller's narrative devices of concealment to external reality may be deduced from the curious public oxymoron of a 'balance of terror': such a euphemism does not conceal nuclear technology's proliferation of new horrors, the development of weapons like the neutron bomb recently created, for instance, which out-rival avant-garde art in breaking with convention and render-ing obsolete all that has come before. Whether one conceives of literature as a strictly determined ideological form or as a cultural product which retains a relative autonomy, its seems probable that such a history of war as continuing literary event informs Heller's novel. Heller's sustained satire against the dullness of maladministration, his post-absurdist lament for the disappearance of identity, suggests that the thrust of war writing in the sixties changed focus, from the heroic struggles of the battlefield to the absurdities of the communi-cations process itself. The strains and confusions endured by American democracy, throughout Korea, the Cold War and McCarthyism[2], seem to have found subliminal articulation in the lunacy of Cathcart, Korn and Major and in the disordered narrative of the novel.

The chief thematic polarity in *Catch-22* is the struggle be-tween the fetishistic, admired and worshipped for itself, and the soldier's counter attempt to hold fast to personal identity. An extended satire upon naming informs the novel at many levels. The case of Major Major Major Major, permanently trapped by his cumbersome names, illustrates such a predica-ment. Major Major, 'born too late and too mediocre', discovers that he is being utterly taken over by 'prolix bulletins', and so he 'grew despondent'. One day he signed Washington Irving's name to a document, an act of rebellion which functioned as catharsis: henceforth he exploits as a counter-strategy the names of other famous writers, notably John Milton, in order to fight back. Of course, Major Major's insubordination brings forth a plethora of activity from security men (whose bizarre activities seem to anticipate fictionally the historical reality of Watergate[3] a decade or so later). The fetishistic status ac-

2. U.S. senator Joseph McCarthy led an anti-Communist witch-hunt in the 1950s.
3. Washington, D.C.'s Watergate Hotel was the scene of a 1970s election scandal that ended in President Richard Nixon's resignation.

Alan Arkin as Yossarian in the 1970 film adaptation of Catch-22. The Kobal Collection.
Reproduced by permission.

corded to trivial memoranda in *Catch-22* signifies an entire
military code, the collective voice of a self-perpetuating bureaucracy whose directives alter consciousness.

Modern war in *Catch-22* appears essentially to be an
administrator's war, the focus having shifted from the exigen-
cies of combat to the rampages of bureaucrats whose methods
of communication imply a new species of epiphenomenalism;
the end result is a situation where the liberal concept of identity is so far eroded that it eventually vanishes altogether. This
finds outstanding comic expression in the novel when literal
truth and the falsified bureaucratic version of reality clash
head-on. Such disjunctures are strewn throughout *Catch-22*,
in the strange figure of the soldier in white, a powerful image
of anonymity, or the unknown soldier Mudd, who, blown to
bits in the sky, generates a persuasive synecdoche [a single
item that symbolizes a whole group] for men at war. The two
most celebrated paradigms are the cases of the dead man in
Yossarian's tent, the soldier who died in a dogfight over Orvi-

eto before he was officially reported missing and is, therefore, deemed never to have died; and the diametrically opposite fate of Doc Daneeka, who is deemed to be dead because he was supposed to be on flight duty in a plane that was destroyed. Doc Daneeka's living presence does nothing to contradict the authorised report of his death. With capacious irony Heller plots the repercussions of his figurative death— for example, the cumulative benefits bestowed upon his 'widow', who eventually refuses to accept his letters, preferring to disown him and accept the official version of his non-existence. The lieutenant who has been killed in action but never officially 'arrived' in the squadron was simply a 'replacement' pilot, whose belongings insist for Yossarian upon the recalcitrance of death, a reality closed to Major Major, who allows Sergeant Towser to report him as never having 'arrived' at all. Such depictions infer the nature of modern war where the substantive reality of combat death often becomes unknowable and its actuality concealed within the labyrinthine processes of modern technology—the circuitry of electronic media, for example—that procedure new kinds of mystification.

The reader of *Catch-22* encounters one of the recurrent preoccupations of American war writers, the domination of combat men by unvalorous administrators. Sergeant Whitcomb, for example, feels delighted that twelve more men have been killed in combat (and they are sent duplicated 'personalised' letters of condolence) because his chances are increased of getting an article in *Saturday Evening Post* in praise of his commanding officer. The war increasingly becomes a publicity man's war where good aerial photographs rather than military tactics dictate the strategy of tight bomb patterns. Language uses, too, assume an important role in the mixed devices of concealment and self-advertisement employed by high-ranking officers: the officers most likely to succeed are those, such as General P.P. Peckem, who are highly sophisticated users of language, or those, such as Scheisskopf, whose crude instrumentation theories and encyclopaedic knowledge of trivial regulations result in promotion to the rank of general. An instance of Scheisskopf's pedantic lunacy occurs in his admiration of parades, the most redundant part of military routine. Beneath Scheisskopf's comic presentation, though, hides a sinister reality; his fixation upon swingless marching hints at a crucifixion mentality. Men, in Scheisskopf's opinion, should ultimately become as precise as machines:

> Lieutenant Scheisskopf's first thought had been to have a friend of his in the sheet metal shop sink pegs of nickel alloy into each man's thighbones and link them to the wrists by strands of copper wire with exactly three inches of play, but there wasn't time—and good copper wire was hard to come by in wartime. He remembered also that the men, so hampered, would be unable to fall properly during the impressive fainting ceremony preceding the marching and that an inability to faint properly might affect the unit's rating as a whole.

Heller's Method Is Neo-Satiric

The literary technique deployed here characterises much of Heller's novel; it sustains awareness, through inventive distortion and departure from strictly literal truth, of the connotations of mechanised slaughter, the transformation of men into machines. As a hospital administrator says to Yossarian on another occasion, when considering the expendability of soldiers, 'one dying boy is just as good as any other or just as bad'. Yossarian learns, too, that his leg 'belongs' to the government.

Heller reveals an aesthetic predilection towards gradual revelation and partial disclosure: for example, the sparse and selective use of conventional literary realism heightens the reader's intuition of aerial combat, acting as a sharper lens. Such naturalistic scenes are framed in the novel, and their locations provide formal interplay within the overall strategy of derangement: they seem almost like set-pieces. The limited usage of 'realistic' presentation is also appropriate in a wider formal sense too, because in the institutionalised world of the novel traditional concepts of worth and epic heroism (which seem to emerge from such realistic presentation) prove obsolete and invalid. The environment of *Catch-22* spawns officers who act not out of moral considerations but only to defend or advance their own interests (as in the ironic promotion of Yossarian for breaking orders). It is wholly consistent, then, that fictional structures and narrative plotting should display a commensurate problematic of evasiveness and disorientation; such a consideration is raised if one examines the relationship of the novel to earlier traditions of war writing. In *Catch-22* many of the familiar conventions of the war novel are transformed into preposterous jokes: even the arrangement of Heller's novel parodies an earlier type of war narrative and movie. The narrative, based on the adventures of a group of officers and men, is broken up into a series of discontinuous sections, each of which only tenuously conveys the experiences of a character, such as Hungry Joe or Nately's Whore. Heller observes few rules in burlesquing the method of earlier naturalistic writers, such as William March in *Company K*, or admired contemporaries, such as Norman Mailer in *The Naked and the Dead*. It is a technique that relies minimally upon plot, and thus allows great organisational flexibility.

Heller's characteristic method may be described as neo-satiric as he frequently shifts the position of attack through a sophisticated usage of fictional apparatus, the deployment of hallucinations, *déjà vu* visions, nightmares, flash-backs and mystical projections that cohere to cloak his characters and ironically imply their occultness in a world where everyday reality seems to imitate the supernatural. Several critics, including Joseph Stern and Brian Way, have written of the symbolic and traditional formulas in Heller's novel. The Soldier in White, for example, parodies the wounded soldier-hero, such as Dalton Trumbo's bandaged protagonist in *Johnny Got His Gun*, and also recalls Shakespeare's ghosts in striking the conscience. This fusion of the neo-satiric, a genre of avant-gardism, with the traditional distinguishes Heller as a war novelist. When Yossarian casts off his uniform and stands naked to receive his undeserved medal he is at one with such earlier deserters and rebels as Frederick Henry [in Ernest Hemingway's *A Farewell to Arms*] or John Andrews [in John Dos Passos's *Three Soldiers*], but when he is absorbed into the Chaplain's mistaken vision, a naked man in a symbolic Tree of Life, he assumes briefly the aura of an Everyman, becoming part of a highly wrought pattern of imagery, like Hungry Joe's cat, which sleeps on his face and finally suffocates him. The planned obsolescence, redundancies and side-tracking in Heller's novel function in a similar manner; the reader can no longer cling to modes and assumptions of a well-tried kind: he finds himself in a satiric environment of constant confusion, and yet one which hints at the apocalyptic only to reemphasise the material and the mundane, the impossibility of spiritual escape.

Catch-22 Is a Parody of Realistic War Novels

David Seed

David Seed is a lecturer in English at the University of Liverpool. He is the author of numerous books and articles on American and British authors.

In the following selection, David Seed suggests that Heller's technique in Catch-22 *of mirroring romantic scenes from the war fiction of Ernest Hemingway, James Jones, and Norman Mailer with absurdly comic scenes has the effect of parodying these earlier novels. However, it is not just war itself that Heller is satirizing but all of government. It is actually the Cold War period of Senator Joseph McCarthy's anticommunism hearings that is the real target of Heller's satire, Seed argues.*

Two preliminary sketches made while Heller was working on *Catch-22* give us important hints of how he originally conceived his protagonist Yossarian. The first begins as follows: 'Now they had just about everything to make a perfect plot for a best-selling war novel. They had a fairy, they had a Slav named Florik from the slums, an Irishman, a thinker with a PhD . . . '. The only character missing from the set is the 'sensitive Jew'. Instead Heller has another Jewish character named Yossarian 'who didn't want to make anything out of anything'. Heller makes the fictional pattern an explicit part of his own narrative, thereby drawing attention to its own fictiveness. On the one hand the sketches make it clear that he was taking his point of departure from the two most famous American novels to deal with the Second World War—*From Here to Eternity* (1951) and *The Naked and the Dead* (1948);

David Seed, "Catch-22," in *The Fiction of Joseph Heller: Against the Grain*, Basingstoke, Hampshire and London: Macmillan Press Ltd., 1989, pp. 22–70. Copyright © 1989 David Seed. Reproduced with permission of Palgrave Macmillan.

on the other it is equally obvious that Heller is not setting out to rival their realism so much as parody many of their procedures. These novels which, according to Heller, delayed the composition of *Catch-22* by years shed light on the nature of his own eventual work.

James Jones treats the army as a microcosm of American society (*From Here to Eternity* is essentially a peacetime novel), stratified and class-ridden. Its two narratives represent failed or abortive attempts to cross divides. Prewitt, like Yossarian, develops a reputation as a trouble-maker and almost wilfully destroys his own army career. The romantic counterpart to this lack of co-operation is his love for a prostitute which comes to an end with the general evacuation of the islands after Pearl Harbor. The second narrative is of Sergeant Warden who falls in love with his company commander's wife. This relationship is not so much doomed as dependent on Warden's willingness to take a commission which, at the last moment, he refuses. Jones's main concern in the novel is to reveal the conservatism and rigidity of the American army which restricts at the same time as it attacks its members. . . .

Parodies Hemingway and Jones

Heller clearly approaches the army in a different way. It is used, he states in a 1976 interview, 'symbolically for the whole government structure.' Given this shift of emphasis from society to administration and his avoidance of the mode of realism which he only sees as a specific limited phase in American fiction from the late 19th century to World War II, we could hardly expect to find a trace of Jones's novel in *Catch-22*. In fact Heller has divided Prewitt's nonconformism and romantic idealism between Yossarian and Nately who falls in love with an Italian prostitute. [Critic] Vance Ramsey has noted the latter similarity between Nately and Prewitt but without pointing out the huge social differences in their origins—Nately from the New England aristocracy, Prewitt from Harlan

County mining area in Kentucky. Warden's affair is repeated briefly by Yossarian with Lieutenant Scheisskopf's wife at training camp, rendered so briefly and ludicrously as to be a parody of *From Here to Eternity*:

> 'Darling, we're going to have a baby again', she would say to Yossarian every month.

> 'You're out of your goddam head', he would reply.

Heller here excludes a possible source of pathos from his own novel. Although the general situation is reminiscent of *From Here to Eternity* the announcement of pregnancy goes even further back to Hemingway's *A Farewell To Arms* and forms a virtual quotation from Chapter 21. Scheisskopf's wife (never named) repeats her monthly phrase to Yossarian *and* to her husband only to be greeted by the latter's own catch-phrase 'Don't you know there's a parade going on?' In both Hemingway's and Jones's novels love functions as a refuge from war or the military, but as a possibility which fails. In *A Farewell To Arms* the notion of a separate peace is ruled out by the interweaving of the two narrative lines. By accelerating tempo Heller increases his parody, contrasting the frenetic pace of *Catch-22* with the futile efforts of Hemingway's characters to slow down the passage of time. Other revisions of *From Here to Eternity* have taken place in *Catch-22*. Jones's Amerindian character Chief Choate becomes Chief Half Whiteoat; and the issue of who runs the mess is blown up into staggering proportions through Heller's mess sergeant Milo Minderbinder. . . .

Heller has described the impact Mailer's novel ('the masterwork') had on him when it first appeared as a daunting one: 'In reading Mailer's work I saw for myself years and years of arduous application, requiring more education than I felt I had. So it had a very prohibiting effect on me'. Partly this was a response to Mailer's craftsmanship, partly an anxiety over the brevity of his own military service.

These reactions help to explain how, years later, Heller as it were purged himself of the oppressive influences of Jones and Mailer, partly by parody and partly by incorporating revised episodes from both novels into his own work. The effect of these revisions is to create an impression of a palimpsest as if Heller were writing over a previous familiar text, exploiting the reader's sense of familiarity so that he can disrupt it in startling ways. The comic treatment of Yossarian's brief affair with Scheisskopf's wife and the intermittent description of his relationship with Nurse Duckett (whose friend Nurse Cramer is as disapproving as [*From Here to Eternity*'s Nurse] Catherine Barkley's companion) distance Heller's own narrative from the novels of Jones and Hemingway; and at the same time they question the possibility of romantic withdrawal from war as a possibility. And Heller's absurd evocation through Orr's 'voyage' to Sweden of the journey up Lake Garda to freedom in *A Farewell To Arms* deals comically (though not dismissively) with the question of escape. The burden of these earlier novels on Heller exactly demonstrates what [literary scholar] Harold Bloom has called the 'anxiety of influence' and parodic allusion in *Catch-22* becomes a means of resisting the authority of these prototexts. Parody and for that matter the whole range of non-realistic techniques used in this novel faced the reader of 1961 with a problem. As John W. Aldridge states, 'most reviewers were locked into a conventional and—as shortly became evident—an outmoded assumption about what war fiction should be. They had, after all, been conditioned by the important novels of World War I and reconditioned by the World War II novels of Norman Mailer, Irwin Shaw, [etc.] . . . to expect that the authentic technique for treating war experience is harshly documentary realism.' On every page *Catch-22* thwarts these expectations and yet, although it does not work within the realistic mode, it does nevertheless insist on the actuality of war and the constant nearness of death. Romance is generally treated as another case of self-delusion; Nately, for instance, is presented as the fool of his own naïveté in falling in love with a whore. When Nelson Algren stated in his review of Heller's novel that the works of Jones and Mailer were 'lost within' it, he was right to pinpoint the influence but wrong to imply that it is concealed. . . .

Yossarian Is an Anti-hero

Initially Yossarian emerges as an anti-hero, comically (but sensibly) devoted to survival: 'his only mission . . . was to come down alive'. His tricks and stratagems to avoid danger (breaking his intercom, checking into the hospital with fake symptoms, etc.) relate his actions to the general direction of the novel's ironies. [Critic] Tony Tanner has rightly commented on the symbolic importance of Yossarian's flying style which physically increases his crew's chances of surviving the flak and which reflects Yossarian's attitude towards the army: 'He is forced to remain within the system, but by his way of moving [ducking and weaving] he can refuse to be of the system, ignoring or negating its rigid patterns'. By defining himself against the system through what he won't do Yossarian becomes a voice of sanity amid the prevailing mania. He is one of the few characters who actually remembers that there is a war going on and who clings on to a residual rationality in spite of the fact that such terms as 'crazy' or 'goofy' are used so often that they almost lose their meaning. . . .

Yossarian's logic represents an effort to detach himself from mass purposes and to rationalise his own individual survival. It makes no difference whether he is shot at by the Germans or by other Americans, or whether he is poisoned by food in the mess. 'Enemy' becomes an umbrella term for all forces trying to kill him, forces which are summarised externally and internally: 'There was Hitler, Mussolini and Tojo, for example, and they were all out to kill him . . . There were lymph glands that might do him in'. Yossarian imagines himself at the focus of a massive conspiracy in a comically exaggerated form of paranoia which might seem ludicrous but which is repeatedly being confirmed by the facts. Towards the end of the novel Nately's whore seems to hold Yossarian guilty for Nately's death and is constantly trying to kill him, moving from place to place with incredible speed and adopting an unbelievable variety of disguises. She realises Yossarian's verbal antics revolve around the most serious topic of all—death. Joking becomes a tactic for recognising death and staving it off briefly by defusing a situation of its sinister implications. The 'death' of the soldier in white becomes an occasion for facetiously accusing the Texan of being a murderer; Yossarian's joke about the German Lepage gun which glues whole formations of planes together temporarily injects comedy into the general fear of bombing Bologna; and so on.

The sort of logic Yossarian uses in the exchange quoted owes a debt to *Alice in Wonderland*, specifically to the dialogue-games with the caterpillar and the Cheshire Cat, and to the why?—why not? question and answer sequence at the mad hatter's tea-party. Yossarian has no monopoly over this kind of argument but uses his skills to telling effect. His arguments question assumptions of patriotic purpose and his joking could be seen as a protective device, an insulating series of performances which buffer him against hostile situations. He performs as the wise fool of the novel, the buffoon whose horseplay conceals a steady resistance to authority for the sanest of reasons—self-preservation. He is particularly quick to identify the roles required of him, as when he is visited by the hospital psychiatrist and starts feeding him the expected lines about his ambivalence, sexual repression, etc. Major Sanderson's refusal to accept his answers (when Yossarian says he dislikes fish because they are too bland he comments 'we'll soon discover the true reason') links the psychiatrist with the administration's general inability to recognise the explicit and obvious—the whole novel is in that respect a sustained assault on common sense—and also discards a possible way of reading the novel through psychological decoding. Yossarian's verbal games then express covert or open defiance of his military superiors and of the administrative procedures to which he is subjected. To a certain extent his sentiments and tactics are endorsed by the narrator who repeatedly injects facetious lines to undermine the decorum of what is being described. When Lieutenant Scheisskopf triumphs in a military parade by training his men not to move their arms, we are told that he won the parade 'hands down'. This appalling joke ties consistently in with Yossarian's hostility towards the pennant prizes for the parades. Heller uses him to set up a Swiftian perspective on them (cf. the ribbons in the Lilliputian court) as empty, meaningless objects. By refusing their symbolism Yossarian is making one of a series of gestures of withdrawal from army values. The most startling example of silent protest is of course his appearance naked to collect a medal after the mission to Avignon. . . .

Yossarian's main problem is how to avoid an early death and Heller has suggested that a development takes place in him towards the 'birth of Yossarian's consciousness of himself as a moral being'. Heller locates the sign of this new awareness as an explicit sense of responsibility to himself. By the end of the novel three options are presented to Yossarian in order to set up his final decision. He could simply stay in hospital, but that would be inconsistent with our sense of Yossarian as a character in motion. Hospital would reduce him to inertia, to a state of passivity associated ultimately with the soldier in white; and anyway hospital does not provide a refuge from death, it simply makes death seem quieter. Yossarian's second option is to accept the deal offered him by Colonels Korn and Cathcart to become a war hero, in effect a PR man for the American army. He accepts this deal and prematurely experiences a surge of exhilaration ('He was home free; he had pulled it off; his act of rebellion had Succeeded . . . '. Here again Heller orders events so that Yossarian's confidence is undercut. The final details of Snowden's death follow this decision which he takes back. Here we come to the third option—to desert. The news of Orr's arrival in Sweden introduces a crucial note of hope into Yossarian's considerations even though the possibility of rowing so far is ludicrous. Throughout the novel Yossarian has been yearning to get to a sanctuary (Majorca, Switzerland and Sweden are mentioned), a symbolic point outside the cycle of corruption and death. The fact that Sweden is so remote and the fact that Yossarian apparently cannot row are irrelevantly realistic considerations to an ambiguous token act. When Yossarian declares that he will 'catch' a ride to Rome and that 'they'll have to try like hell to catch me this time'; and when he 'takes off' in the last line of the novel Heller has revised two of the book's key terms so as to suggest liberation from the entrapment which has beset Yossarian throughout. But his escape remains a matter of nuance and ambiguous suggestion. Almost any discussion of the ending makes it sound more positive than the text would warrant. . . .

Catch-22 and the McCarthy Era

Whatever the exact nature of the novel he began around 1945 Heller clearly made a fresh start in 1953. Again and again in interviews he has insisted that the true subject of *Catch-22* was contemporary and that it was only obliquely about the last World War: 'I regard this essentially as a peacetime book. What distresses me very much is that the ethic often dictated by a wartime emergency has a certain justification, but when this thing is carried *over* into areas of peace; where the same demands are made upon the individual in the cause of national interest . . . this wartime emergency ideology transplanted to peacetime leads not only to absurd situations, but to very tragic situations'. One of the most striking indications of transposed emphasis in the novel is how little attention is

Montgomery Clift and Donna Reed in a scene from the 1953 movie From Here to Eternity. AP Images.

paid to the Germans. As Heller later explained, 'it's essentially a conflict between people—American officers and their own government. They are the antagonists of *Catch-22*—much more so than the Germans and Hitler, who are scarcely mentioned'. The vocabulary of battle is transferred to the American air force exclusively, thereby forcing the reader to revise his sense of sides and to locate characters within the American power structures. Quasi-military manoeuvres become utterly self-serving (Colonel Cathcart is an 'industrious, intense, dedicated military tactician who calculated day and night in the service of himself') or a reflex to opposition from fellow-officers. General Peckem redefines strategic objectives to Lieutenant Scheisskopf as an effort to take over every other bomber group and the one enemy he indicates on his map board is General Dreedle. Threat is internalised into one's own army and then internalised again into private fears and uncertainties; Cathcart, for instance, wavers between extremes of confidence and terror.

An all-pervading atmosphere of paranoia spreads through the novel, a suspicion of potential anonymous enemies referred to collectively as 'them'. Here Heller anticipates reactions to the Vietnam War. [Novelist] Philip Roth has recorded that during this period 'one even began to use the word "America" as though it was the name . . . of a foreign invader that had conquered the country and with whom one refused, to the best of one's strength and ability, to collaborate. Suddenly America had turned into "them"'. The alienation Roth describes finds its equivalent in Heller's use of anachronisms which, as we shall see in a moment, make it impossible to read the novel as a realistic account of events towards the end of World War II. The reader can neither naturalise the setting nor the period of its action since it incorporates material from two very different eras. In that sense Heller's revision of the name of the novel's island setting from Corsica to Pianosa is a symptomatic shift away from realistic description.

Heller creates ludicrous comedy out of the surveillance practised by the CID [Criminal Investigation Department] officers whose disguises are transparently obvious, and who even start investigating each other. As usual in the novel comic possibilities develop a more sinister edge where the forces represented by these officers are no longer out in the open. Nurse Duckett warns Yossarian of a conversation she overheard behind a closed door, that 'they' are going to 'disappear' his friend Dunbar, and sure enough Dunbar vanishes. The constant references to conspiracy relate the novel to postwar America. As Heller has stated, 'it was the America of the Cold War I wrote about, the Rosenberg trials, the McCarthy hearings, the loyalty oaths'. . . .

Minderbinder as Postwar Profiteering

Through the figure of Milo Minderbinder Heller parodies the postwar profiteering impulse which swept through America on its new wave of prosperity. In 1975 he explained that he had drawn Milo from at least one specific figure: '... when Milo Minderbinder says, "what's good for Milo Minderbinder is good for the country", he's paraphrasing Charles E. Wilson, the former head of General Motors, who told a Senate committee, "what is good for the country is good for General Motors, and vice versa"'. Although Milo is a parodic figure Heller took care to avoid a 'bloated plutocrat stereotype' and created instead a personification of commercial activity. It is crucial that Milo speaks in slogans—sometimes his own, sometimes borrowed from Benjamin Franklin (on the value of thrift) or from Calvin Coolidge ('the business of government is business'). These slogans are self-promoting and also identify Milo with a tradition of national enterprise. Within himself he encapsulates the history of capitalism from its early stage of individual production (one of Milo's first deals produces a quarter of a bed-sheet as 'profit'!) to its modern extension into international cartels. . . .

Milo's enterprises represent the sort of commercial enterprises associated with peacetime accelerated, expanded and transposed on to the theatre of war. War heightens the cynicism and hypocrisy involved in the deals. Like [Thomas Pynchon's] *Gravity's Rainbow*, *Catch-22* exploits historical retrospection to show a continuity between the novel's ostensible subject (the last stages of World War II) and its investigation of contemporary America. Both Pynchon and Heller insert anachronisms into their texts to break open their fictitious time. . . .

Heller Superimposes Cold War Era on WW II

Alienation is in fact the crucial cumulative effect of Heller's anachronisms and parodies. In chronological terms he forces the reader to superimpose one period (the 1950s) on another (1944) as if in mimicry of Joseph McCarthy's paranoid rereading of American military history. A continuity is thus implied between a period of warfare and one of peace—at least one of *ostensible* peace since the Cold War could be seen as a time of latent warfare. By burlesquing the key trials of the postwar period Heller uses absurdist techniques to bring to the surface the hidden ideological assumptions of the McCarthy era: its paranoia, xenophobia, racism and general preoccupation with secrecy. The novel repeatedly converts conspiracy into comic theatre as if Heller's characters were performing in an endless farce, where the momentum of their own activities acts as the justification of those activities and obscures the most obvious realities of their situation. In the course of an excellent discussion of nonsense literature Elizabeth Sewell offers the following summary:

> I am going to describe something—a system, call it a political system . . . These are some of its traits: (1) it is ruled by an obsessive logic, starting from principles that may be inhuman or absurd but are to be rigidly followed; (2) those within the system are compelled to work with it not by external force so much as by the sheer compulsion of logic on the human mind; (3) the system is totally insulated from all that we agree to regard as normal life; (4) it requires nonsensical tasks to be performed; (5) each individual within it is isolated from every other, by a policy of propaganda, control, and terror.

It would be difficult to imagine a more concise summary of the political nature of the system in *Catch-22*. In almost every respect Sewell's description matches the self-perpetuating, insulated logic which guides the military bureaucracy and, as if that wasn't enough, Sewell draws parallels between such a system and the McCarthy hearings as well as other developments in postwar America. By showing such absurdities Heller's humour performs a political function, since it brings to the surface the implicit assumptions of a right-wing, Cold War mentality and in that respect *Catch-22* looks forward to Heller's subsequent writings of the 1960s.

Catch-22 Is an Antiwar Novel of the 1950s

Josh Greenfeld

Josh Greenfeld is an author and screenwriter best known for his screenplay for the movie Harry and Tonto. *He is also the author of three books about his autistic son, including* A Child Called Noah.

In this retrospective analysis of Catch-22 *that appeared seven years after its publication, Josh Greenfeld quotes Joseph Heller as saying that Vietnam was the war he had in mind when he wrote his first novel,* Catch-22. *Greenfeld takes exception to Heller's remarks, arguing that the spirit of* Catch-22 *is much more akin to the spirit of the acquiescent 1950s—as typified by the power possessed by Senator Joseph McCarthy in his anticommunism crusade—than that of the turbulent 1960s, when the escalating Vietnam War provoked significant social resistance.*

Some novels appear ahead of their time, others come out at just the right time, but only a very few seem to belong to any, or all, time. It would appear ... that "Catch-22," by Joseph Heller, is making a strong bid to transcend its own time. A recent revisit to the heady island of Pianosa has impressed on me, as I admit I suspected it might, how much more germane—and more darkly hilarious—the novel seems today than it did when it was published in October, 1961. Yet I was also struck by the extent to which either it or I have aged.

The Bible of Sixties

In case you've forgotten, or never knew, "Catch-22" is the story of Yossarian, the Assyrian World War II bombardier with the Armenian name, a Jewish Talmudic mind, an all-American heart, and the irresolution of the most famous Dane [i.e., Hamlet]. Yossarian "has decided to live forever or die in the attempt and his only mission each time he went up was to come down alive."

Yossarian always views the war with himself at the center of the big picture in a zoom-lens close-up. But though he desperately wants out, he always comes up against the unremitting logical non-reason of military bureaucracy: anyone who is crazy must be grounded; anyone who is willing to fly combat missions must be crazy; ergo, anyone who flies should be grounded. But, in order to be grounded it is required that one request grounding; no one crazy enough to fly missions would ask; and if one should, "there's a catch . . . Catch-22. Anyone who wants to get out of combat duty isn't really crazy." Ergo, no exit, except by way of the casualty lists.

There seems no denying that though Heller's macabre farce was written about a rarefied part of the raging war of the forties during the silent fifties, it has all but become the chapbook of the sixties. . . .

Heller Had Vietnam War in Mind

[Heller attributes the emergence of "Catch-22" as a popular classic] to three reasons, which he checks off on his fingers as efficiently as a broker explaining the potentialities of a growth stock:

"First, it's a great book. I've come to accent the verdict of the majority.

"Second, a whole new generation of readers is being introduced to it, the generation that was 11 or 12 when it first came out.

"Third, and most important: Vietnam. Because that was the war I had in mind; a war fought without military provocation, a war in which the real enemy is no longer the other side but someone allegedly on your side. The ridiculous war I felt lurking in the future when I wrote the book. So 'Catch-22' certainly has more meaning in regard to Vietnam than World War II."

Heller is unquestionably right that the world of Pianosa is closer to Danang than Sardinia, but I don't think the novel is as contemporary as it seems. Rereading "Catch-22" it struck me that its origins and ambience lie in between the forties and the sixties—in the decade when Heller conceived and wrote it. For if the fifties can be characterized as the age of acquiescence, when whispered demurral amounted to near-heroic protest in the face of Senator [Joseph] McCarthy's assault on the left (strange to recall that [McCarthy-opposing attorney] Joseph Welch and [McCarthy critic and journalist] Edward R. Murrow were our heroes), then "Catch-22" belongs more to that decade than to the present one [the 1960s], when active protest has emerged in such relatively extreme forms as draft resistance and military desertion.

A Novel of the Fifties

For while the theme of "Catch-22" is a variation of what Norman Mailer has called "exquisite totalitarianism" as it applies to the military, its implementation—though it is at once as intricately complicated and precise as a medieval tapestry, as slapstick as a Keystone Kops chase, as fast-moving as a cinema verité film—remains curiously static. The characters are almost all caricatures, in an arrested state, at least up to the point of death, when they seem to dress for the occasion by assuming flesh. And Yossarian himself—the novel's central character and spine—though he appears to be Heller's attempt to create a cosmopolitan "everyman," is really more like a plain nobody. For he essentially lacks bedrock character—hard and individual substance; actions rub against his character rather than his character being the hard cutting edge that delineates actions.

In fact, by identifying with Yossarian the would-be rebel can remain the would-be rebel. Caught up in motion—and emotion—as he glides along the establishment tracks, he can avoid coming to grips with the implications of the movements and actions of the real rebel who has character enough to make his own tracks. With Yossarian's obedience, his commitment to and unwillingness to confront the organization that is out to destroy him (for instance, he cannot lend his sanction to a buddy's proposal to assassinate the C.O.), his personal and nonideological opposition to war, he best represents a case-study example of the kind of liberal mentality—or sentimentality—that must proceed to great neurotic lengths of mental gymnastics before being able to step off the curb and take one self-committing baby step into the street.

That is why, I think, the ending of "Catch-22"—when Yossarian finally decides to desert—seems flat and unconvincing. It is the result of a repetition of process rather than an expression of character, giving the reader, at least in retrospect, the disappointing sensation of having observed a great deal of warm-up exercise just to witness the lifting of a five-pound barbell.

That Yossarian learns the hard way what a more substantial character might have started out knowing was, I should in fairness point out, a great argument for the book when it came out, and it can be used as even a greater argument today. It is, in fact, Heller's argument. But I still cannot help believing that to structure an anti-war novel upon a base implicitly requiring one to view war as a learning process or a game is a mistake, for it is to fall into the trap that leads to the glamorization of war itself. The tendency to do so was a hangover from World War II that many of us suffered in the fifties (a hangover which helped to put one of the war's heroes in the White House [i.e., Eisenhower]), but there are hopeful signs that it is passé in the sixties.

What diverts the reader of "Catch-22" from the conclusion that it is really a fifties cop-out is, of course, Heller's marvelous technical ability to create suspense by playfully promising significant jigsaw pieces to complete puzzles that—like Yossarian's character—do not really exit. And while Heller's blackly humorous ability may also be a fossil of the forlorn fifties—when cool humor in the face of despair was the style—it is still astonishingly effective, possibly the best example of its kind. I mean that I found the antic humor of "Catch-22" still robustly fresh, still side-splittingly funny. I know of no book written in the last twenty years that continues to make me laugh out loud so much. So if I must conclude that it is not a great book—whatever that means—and not as bold, far-out and venturesome as it pretends to be, I still think it is a major work.

Catch-22 Is About the Cold War and the Korean War

Ken Barnard

Ken Barnard was a reporter for the Detroit News.

In this interview with reporter Ken Barnard, Joseph Heller states that Catch-22 *is more about the Korean War and the Cold War than about World War II. Heller goes on to say that his personal feelings about World War II were different than Yossarian's: Heller was supportive of the war. Heller tells Barnard that in* Catch-22, *he was depicting a government at war with its own people—a theme that emerged from events during the Korean and Cold Wars.*

People are always asking Heller, who flew 60 missions as a World War II bombardier, why he waited until 1953 to begin the novel about the hapless Yossarian and his zany bombers.

His reply: "I started the book when I was ready. There's a line in Samuel Beckett's *Endgame* when he asks his parents, 'Why did you have me?' and the father replies, 'We didn't know it would be you.' I didn't have *Catch-22* to write until I began writing it. It's not as though I postponed writing that particular novel until 1953 when I had the idea and began it. I don't think I could have written or even conceived it right after the war.

Conflict Between People and Their Government

"What *Catch-22* is more about than World War II is the Korean War and the Cold War. The elements that inspired the ideas came to me from the civilian situation in this country in

Ken Barnard, "Interview with Joseph Heller," *Detroit News*, September 13, 1970, pp. 19, 24, 27–28, 30, 65. Copyright © 1970 *The Detroit News*, a Gannett newspaper. Reproduced with permission of *The Detroit News*.

the 1950's when we did have such things as loyalty oaths to say when we were at war in Korea and [General Douglas] MacArthur did seem to be wanting to provoke a war against China, when [U.S. secretary of state John Foster] Dulles was taking us to the brink of war against Russia every other week and it seemed inevitable that we were going to plunge right into another major war.

"Until that time we were in a process of restoring ourselves. The same factionalism, the same antagonism, the mortal enmity that exists between groups today in this country existed then as well. But to me it was a new phenomenon. I chose the war (World War II) as a setting because it seemed to me we were at war. Certainly that was the start of the civil rights movement, for example. There were whites who wanted to kill every black. I remember those really disgustingly terrifying photographs of little children going to school in Clinton, Ky., and New Orleans—little black kids going into kindergarten and those white monsters with clubs—the women snarling and cursing and their faces contorted by such hatred.

"Then there was the same type of antagonism developing between (Senator) Joseph McCarthy—and Nixon and his committee—and people who, well, it then was called the Communist conspiracy. Teachers and Quakers were being fired. There was a kind of war going on between groups.

"I see *Catch-22* as not about World War II. It certainly does not reflect my attitude toward that war. For everybody after Pearl Harbor, it was a war we wanted to fight—a war we knew had to be won. It doesn't reflect my emotions of combat, which were different from Yossarian's. An important point in the book is that the war in Europe is drawing to a close as the danger to Yossarian from his own superiors intensifies. He was able to say in the end of the book that the war against Germany is just about over and the country's not in danger any more, but he is. It's essentially a conflict between people— American officers and their own government. They are the antagonists of *Catch-22*—much more so than the Germans and Hitler, who are scarcely mentioned.

"The combat men found themselves at the mercy of the people who are employed to serve them, the administrators. In order to get their flak suits they have to sing the Star-Spangled Banner twice; in order to get the maps they have to recite the Pledge of Allegiance; and they suddenly find themselves enslaved by those officials whose original function was to be of service to them.

"I think we've had such a situation continuing since the end of World War II, and the novel applies even more today [in 1970]."

Heller believed he was distorting ridiculous systems of logic that an entrenched officialdom can hatch. The symbolic novel he thought he was writing has been transformed by ensuing events into a realistic novel. A propos of the development, he summons a wry smile as he asks: "Remember reading in the papers about this general and the master sergeants who were investigated for watering [down] PX (post exchange [soldiers' general store]) booze and sending money into Switzerland?" The smile becomes a hearty laugh as he adds: "To me the funniest part is that they took back their medals!"

Heller Described His Own Experiences in *Catch-22*

For 15 years after the war it was impossible to persuade Heller to get aboard an airplane. He still thinks you have "to be nuts or have a potential for being nuts to become a pilot."

He flew more than 20 missions before he saw a plane shot down with men bailing out. "Till then it was a lark. Even when the missions were dangerous, I was too stupid to realize it. It was like a movie to me."

It was his 37th mission—his second to Avignon—which is described in the book and movie and left him looking forward passionately to becoming an ex-flier. During it, the co-

Jon Voight and Alan Arkin in a scene from the 1970 film adaptation of Catch-22. The Kobal Collection. Reproduced by permission.

pilot went "a little berserk" and grabbed the controls away from the pilot. Heller was in the nose of the bomber and did not know what had happened. For a while he felt they had lost a wing and were going straight down. He had just seen an engine blow up on the aircraft ahead of his ship with a wing falling off, the plane going down and no parachutes coming out.

"Then suddenly after we dropped our bombs," he says, "our plane started to go straight down and I was pinned to the top of the cabin. The co-pilot had thought we were climbing too steeply and would stall. He grabbed the controls to shove us back down. We went down and I thought I was dying.

"Then the plane straightened out and flew through flak and my earphones were pulled out. I didn't know my headset was out. You know, when you press the button to talk, you hear a click, but I pressed it and heard nothing, so I thought I was already dead.

"For a while the rest of the crew couldn't hear me, and when I did plug in I heard this guy—the co-pilot—hysterical on the intercom yelling, 'The bombardier doesn't answer. Help him! Help him! Go help the bombardier.' And I said, 'I'm the bombardier; I'm OK,' and he said, 'Go help the gunner.' He was shot through the leg and that's in the book and movie. But I added to it and had him shot in the middle."

Heller made a promise to himself that if he survived the war he would stay off airplanes. For years he was true to his word. Then he spent 24 hours on a train from Miami to New York—"and that's when I changed my mind: I decided I'd rather be dead."

Catch-22 Is About World War II

Michael C. Scoggins

Michael C. Scoggins is a research historian with the York County Culture and Heritage Commission in York County, South Carolina. He is the author of several articles and books, including The Day It Rained Militia: Huck's Defeat and the Revolution in the South Carolina Backcountry, May–July 1780.

In the following selection, Michael C. Scoggins argues that Joseph Heller's combat experiences played a much greater role in the creation of Catch-22 *than has been acknowledged by most critics. He points out parallels between Heller's actual wartime experiences and the storyline and details of* Catch-22. *As in* Catch-22, *Heller found that the number of missions required of aircrews before being rotated home kept increasing. The central event in* Catch-22—*the death of Snowden on the Avignon mission—parallels a traumatic Avignon mission Heller endured.*

In the forty-one years since the initial publication of *Catch-22*, Joseph Heller's best-selling 1961 novel about World War II, the book has been a favorite subject for analysis and commentary, and an enormous body of literary criticism on the work has been published. There have been numerous essays on the novel's structure, its debt to other works of literature, its humor and logic, its moral and ethical values, and its religious themes and mythical overtones. However, Heller's treatment of the war itself has received scant attention by most critics. [The] majority of Heller's critics have taken the stance that *Catch-22* has very little to do with World War II and is in fact not a war novel at all. Heller himself consistently mini-

Michael C. Scoggins, "Joseph Heller's Combat Experiences in *Catch-22*," *War, Literature & the Arts*, vol. 15, nos. 1 & 2, 2003, pp. 213–21. Copyright © 2003 by Michael C. Scoggins. Reproduced by permission of the author.

mized the war's influence on the novel in many of his statements and interviews. For instance, in a 1970 speech in New York City, he told his audience that "*Catch-22* is not really about World War II", and in a 1975 interview he reiterated those sentiments: "As I've said, *Catch-22* wasn't really *about* World War Two. It was really about American society during the Cold War, during the Korean War, and about the possibility of a Vietnam."

Heller Used His Own Combat Experiences in *Catch-22*

Thus it is not surprising to find that very few critics have actually studied the characters and plot elements in *Catch-22* that Heller borrowed from his own experiences as an Army Air Force bombardier. In this essay I will demonstrate that Heller's military career played a much greater role in the concept and structure of *Catch-22* than most critics have ever suspected. Many of the characters and incidents in *Catch-22* were in fact drawn directly from Heller's tour of duty, and were simply modified or exaggerated for dramatic effect. . . .

Joseph Heller was a nineteen-year-old Jewish-American from Brooklyn, New York when he enlisted in the US Army Air Corps in 1942; his three years of military service included a tour of duty as a wing bombardier in the Mediterranean theater of operations. From early May 1944 until December 1944, he was stationed on the island of Corsica where he flew sixty combat missions in B-25 "Mitchell" bombers with the 488th Bombardment Squadron, 340th Bombardment Group, 57th Bombardment Wing, 12th Air Force. Like Yossarian's fictional 27th Air Force, the real 12th Air Force was engaged in flying tactical support missions over northern Italy and southern France. After Heller completed his required quota of missions, the Air Force rotated him back to the States under the point system in December 1944. . . .

While most *Catch-22* readers will remember Captain John Yossarian as a man who is deathly afraid of being killed and who wants out of combat at all costs, it is clear that at the beginning of the war he was as patriotic as anyone else. . . .

In his 1975 interview, Heller revealed his own feelings at the beginning of the war. "I actually *hoped* I would get into combat," he related. "I was just 19 and there were a great many movies being made about the war; it all seemed so dramatic and heroic. . . . I saw it as a war of necessity. Everybody did. . . . Pearl Harbor united this country in a strong and wholesome and healthy way." Later in the same interview, he reaffirmed his belief that World War II was a necessary war. "It offended some people, during the Vietnam war, that I had not written a truly pacifist book." . . . "But I am not a true pacifist. World War Two was necessary at least to the extent that we were fighting for the survival of millions of people." Heller also made it clear that Yossarian's views about the war were not his own: "Yossarian's emotions, Yossarian's reaction to the war in the squadron were not those I experienced when I was overseas."

During the course of the novel, two important catalysts are responsible for changing Yossarian's attitude towards flying combat. The first is the continually increasing number of missions that the men are required to fly. When Yossarian first arrives in Europe, the airmen are required to complete only twenty-five missions before being rotated home. In order to impress his superiors, the fanatical group commander, Colonel Cathcart, raises the number of missions from twenty-five to thirty, and he continues to increase the number in increments of five, until by the end of the novel the men are required to fly eighty missions before they can go home. . . .

The number of mission required of the aircrews in *Catch-22* is an accurate reflection of the reality of the war in southern Europe. In northern Europe, the crews of the 8th Air Force's B-17 and B-24 heavy strategic bombers flew deep into

Germany and were often in the air for eight to ten hours at a time. Until long-range escort fighters like the P-51 "Mustang" became available late in the war, they suffered terrible losses from German fighters and antiaircraft fire. As a consequence, for most of the war the B-17 and B-24 crews were required to fly only twenty-five missions before being rotated home. In comparison, the shorter range B-25s in southern Europe flew missions lasting for only a few hours, and they often flew several missions per day. As Heller noted in his autobiography, his quota was raised several times during his own tour. When he arrived in Corsica in early 1944, the number of missions for his group was up to fifty, and during his tour it went from fifty to fifty-five, and then to sixty. By the time he was taken off combat status, the number of required missions had reached seventy. . . .

Heller's Mission over Avignon

It is over Avignon that Yossarian experiences the other catalytic moment in his tour of duty, an episode that absolutely terrifies him and that makes him realize he might not survive the war after all. This mission over Avignon is referred to in ever increasing detail throughout the novel, as Heller gradually reveals more and more about the experience until, near the end of the novel, we finally come to understand just what it is that drives Yossarian to feel the way he does.

Yossarian's pilot on the Avignon mission is Lieutenant Huple. Although Huple is a good pilot, he is also a fifteen-year-old kid who has enlisted illegally—a fact that does not exactly inspire confidence among his fellow airmen. The copilot is Yossarian's friend Dobbs, and in the rear of the plane is a young radio operator/turret gunner named Snowden. Early in the novel Heller tells us that "Snowden had been killed over Avignon when Dobbs went crazy in mid-air and seized the controls away from Huple." Later, we learn more about this mission "when Dobbs went crazy in mid-air and began weeping pathetically for help":

> "Help him, help him," Dobbs sobbed. "Help him, help him."

> "Help who? Help who?" called back Yossarian, once he had plugged his headset back into the intercom system, after it had been jerked out when Dobbs wrested the controls away from Huple and hurled them all down suddenly into the deafening, paralyzing, horrifying dive which had plastered Yossarian helplessly to the ceiling of the plane by the top of his head and from which Huple had rescued them just in time by seizing the controls back from Dobbs and leveling the ship out almost as suddenly right back in the middle of the buffeting layer of cacophonous flak from which they had escaped successfully only a moment before. *Oh, God! Oh, God, oh God*, Yossarian had been pleading wordlessly as he dangled from the ceiling on the nose of the ship by the top of his head, unable to move.

> "The bombardier, the bombardier," Dobbs answered in a cry when Yossarian spoke. "He doesn't answer, he doesn't answer. Help the bombardier, help the bombardier."

> "I'm the bombardier," Yossarian cried back at him. "I'm the bombardier. I'm all right. I'm all right."

> "Then help him, help him," Dobbs begged. "Help him, help him."

About midway through the novel, Heller gives us some more details, telling us that the Avignon mission "was the mission on which Yossarian lost his nerve." After several subsequent references to "Snowden's secret," which serve to build up the reader's suspense and anticipation, Heller finally gives us the rest of the story, and we find out the true nature of this "secret." After Huple regains control of the aircraft, Yossarian crawls to the back of the plane to check on the wounded gunner. Snowden is lying in the back of the aircraft with a large gash in one of his thighs, caused by a piece of flak that tore through the side of the plane and cut into his leg. Behind him, the tail gunner is on the floor in a "dead faint," having passed out from the shock of seeing Snowden's wound. Yossarian treats the wound as best he can with a first-aid kit and tries to reassure the wounded gunner, who keeps complaining, "I'm cold, I'm cold." When Yossarian opens up Snowden's flak suit to look for another wound, Snowden's "secret" becomes apparent: a second piece of flak has torn into Snowden's body from the other side, and as Yossarian unzips his suit, Snowden's intestines spill out onto the floor of the aircraft in a "soggy pile."

As Heller was to reveal in later interviews and his autobiography, this incident was a synthesis of several of his own combat experiences. . . .

[It] was Heller's second mission over Avignon, on 15 August 1944, that provided most of the details for the Snowden incident in *Catch-22*. For both Yossarian and Heller, it was their thirty-seventh mission. As the B-25s approached the target, the German antiaircraft fire was once again accurate and deadly. As his squadron began its bomb run, a B-25 in another squadron was hit by flak and one of its wings broke off. The plane nosed over and plunged to earth, and none of the crew escaped. Two other planes also went down during the mission, again with no survivors. Heller's squadron dropped their bombs and then quickly banked up and away from the target. He describes what happened next in *Now and Then*:

> And then the bottom of the plane just seemed to drop out: we were falling, and I found myself pinned helplessly to the top of the bombardier's compartment, with my flak helmet squeezed against the ceiling. What I did not know (it was reconstructed for me later) was that one of the two men at the controls, the copilot, gripped by the sudden fear that our plane was about to stall, seized the controls to push

them forward and plunged us into a sharp descent, a dive, that brought us back down into the level of the flak.

I had no power to move, not even a finger. And I believed with all my heart and quaking soul that my life was ending and that we were going down, like the plane on fire I had witnessed plummeting only a few minutes before. I had no time for anything but terror. And then just as suddenly—I think I would have screamed had I been able to—we leveled out and began to climb away again from the flak bursts, and now I was flattened against the floor, trying frantically to grasp something to hold on to when there was nothing. And in another few seconds we were clear and edging back into formation with the rest of the planes. But as I regained my balance and my ability to move, I heard in the ears of my headphones the most unnatural and sinister of sounds: silence, dead silence. And I was petrified again. Then I recognized, dangling loosely before me, the jack to my headset. It had been torn free from the outlet. When I plugged myself back in, a shrill bedlam of voices was clamoring in my ears, with a wail over all the rest repeating on the intercom that the bombardier wasn't answering. "The bombardier doesn't answer!" "I'm the bombardier," I broke in immediately. "And I'm all right." "Then go back and help him, help the gunner. He's hurt."

Heller made his way to the rear of the airplane and found the radio gunner lying on the floor with a large oval wound in his thigh; a piece of flak had punched through the side of the plane and torn open the gunner's leg, just as recounted in *Catch-22*. Fighting down his own nausea at the sight of the wound, Heller poured sulfa powder into the cut, bandaged it and gave the gunner a shot of morphine. When the young man began to complain of feeling cold, Heller reassured him that they would be home soon and that he would be all right. Once the plane landed, the wounded gunner was taken to the base hospital and eventually made a full recovery. It was apparently this action that netted Heller his Air Medal. Heller took the rest of the Snowden story, the part about the horrible intestinal wound, from an incident that occurred on an earlier mission over Ferrara, Italy, on 16 July 1944. A radio gunner in Heller's squadron, Sergeant Vandermeulen, had his midsection sliced open by a burst of flak and died in the back of his aircraft, moaning that he was cold. "For my episodes of Snowden in the novel," Heller stated, "I fused the knowledge of that tragedy with the panicked copilot and the thigh wound to the top turret gunner in my own plane on our second mission to Avignon." After this mission, Heller came away with a new appreciation of the dangers of combat:

> I might have seemed a hero and been treated as something of a small hero for a short while, but I didn't feel like one. They were trying to kill me, and I wanted to go home. That they were trying to kill all of us each time we went up was no consolation. They were trying to kill *me*.

> I was frightened on every mission after that one, even the certified milk runs. It could have been about then that I began crossing my fingers each time we took off and saying in silence a little prayer. It was my sneaky ritual. . . .

La Spezia Mission Drawn from Heller's Experiences

Many of Heller's other combat experiences round their way into *Catch-22*, including a mission to bomb an Italian ship that is recounted almost identically in both his novel and his autobiography. As Heller tells the story in *Catch-22*:

> Intelligence had reported that a disabled Italian cruiser in drydock at La Spezia would be towed by the Germans that same morning to a channel at the entrance of the harbor and scuttled there to deprive the Allied armies of deep-water port facilities when they captured the city. For once, a military intelligence report proved accurate. The long vessel was halfway across the harbor when they [Yossarian's bomb

group] flew in from the west, and they broke it apart with direct hits from every flight that filed them all with waves of enormously satisfying group pride until they found themselves engulfed in great barrages of flak that rose from guns in every bend of the huge horseshoe of mountainous land below.

In the novel, Yossarian's friends Dobbs and Nately are both killed on the mission to La Spezia. Heller's description of this mission in his autobiography is virtually identical to the account in *Catch-22*, with one important exception: although there was heavy flak, none of his friends were killed. He tells us that this mission, one of the last he flew, filled him with both "military and civilian pride, the civilian pride bred of my sole assertion of leadership and authority as an officer." The La Spezia mission was flown on 23 September 1944 to destroy the Italian cruiser *Taranto*, and the 340th Bomb Group won its second Presidential Distinguished Unit Citation for this mission, a citation in which Heller shared. As he relates in *Now and Then*:

> The assignment that morning was a hurried one. The destination was the large Italian seaport of La Spezia. The target was an Italian cruiser reportedly being towed out into a deep channel of the harbor by the Germans, to be scuttled there as an obstacle to approaching Allied ground forces pressing steadily north. . . . When I looked behind us after we had flown through the flak at La Spezia and turned off, I was greatly satisfied with myself and all that I saw, and with all the others as well. We were unharmed; the turbulent oceans of dozens and dozens of smutty black clouds from the countless flak bursts were diffused all over the sky at different heights. The other flights were coming through without apparent damage. And down below I could watch the bombs from one cascade after another exploding directly on the ship that was our target.

Catch-22 Prepared Us for the Vietnam War

John Clark Pratt

John Clark Pratt was a professor of English at Colorado State University. He has written and edited numerous books about the Vietnam War era, including The Laotian Fragments *and* Vietnam Voices: Perspectives on the War Years, 1941–1982.

In the following selection, John Clark Pratt, a Vietnam veteran, finds so many parallels between the Vietnam War and Catch-22 *that he argues the book should be considered a paradigm for that war. He finds many examples of official lunacy in his Vietnam experiences that directly parallel scenes from* Catch-22. *Pratt concludes that having read* Catch-22 *made him better able to cope with the surrealism of the Vietnam War.*

At the outset, I must confess to some unintentional skullduggery. When going to Vietnam in the summer of 1969, I took with me a copy of *Catch-22*. From what I knew then about the war, I suspected that reviewing the plight of Yossarian from time to time might provide some continued reassurance that my world at war would not really be any more insane than Joseph Heller's.

I could not know, of course, that the colonel seated next to me throughout that long, ominous flight would comment on my choice of fiction and provide me with some early material for my novel, *The Laotian Fragments*. In *Fragments*, Major Bill Blake also reads *Catch-22* on the flight over, and when the colonel asks about the book (obviously not having heard of it), Blake tells him only that it is "a novel about World War

II." Returning for his second tour, the colonel observes, "That was a real war . . . not like this one. Later, Blake signs many of his official memos "Love, Yossarian."

The Paradoxes of *Catch-22* and Vietnam

Naturally, those of us who knew *Catch-22* could not help but see some obvious parallels to Vietnam, and almost all of them involved the fact of conflicting realities that lie at the core of Heller's vision of the modern world. Vietnam was a "conflict" that was neither a war nor a Korean "police action." In Vietnam, many of us became involved in operations that we could not talk about, even to people who were also involved in often contiguous operations that they couldn't talk about either. We discovered that the war had been going on longer than even many of the senior commanders knew and that it was being fought in and by countries that professed neutrality and non-involvement. What FNG (F--king New Guy) who knew *Catch-22* could help but wonder, when visiting either the Saigon exchanges or the stalls in Cholon, where Milo Minderbinder might be? And who of us can ever forget the sense of incredible irony when we exited the aircraft that had brought us to Vietnam and heard the phrase that only Heller could have written, spoken perfunctorily by an obviously veteran stewardess: "Hope you enjoyed your flight. See you in a year."

General comparisons are one thing, but the unreal reality, the actuality of *Catch-22* provided specifics as well to all of us who knew the novel—so many, so often and so incredibly true that the book should properly be seen as a paradigm for the Vietnam War itself. When looking at the "facts" as well as at the fiction written about the war, to ignore what Heller has written is to obfuscate, misunderstand, and more dangerously, I think, distort what the Vietnam experience really was.

Let us look first at the "fact," then at the fiction. In *Dispatches*, Michael Herr said it best: "You couldn't avoid the way in which things got mixed, the war itself with those parts of the war that were just like the movies, just like *The Quiet American* or *Catch-22* (a Nam standard because it said that in a war everybody thinks that everybody else is crazy). . . ." It's Yossarian, of course, who tells the chaplain, "Everybody is crazy but us," a feeling that I know was held by many of the pilots who flew north from Thailand (a country *not* at war) into the Red River Valley or against the Thanh Hoa bridge, taking the same routes at the same times day after day, experiencing ever-increasing flak from antiaircraft artillery and surface-to-air missile [SAM] sites that had been off-limits for enough time to allow the North Vietnamese to make them operational. Still classified, for instance, are the details about a senior officer's being relieved of command because he authorized and planned an attack against SAM sites under construction, but just as the armed aircraft were readying for takeoff, the mission was canceled from Washington. In all this, one recalls Milo's having alerted the German antiaircraft artillery in order to "be fair to both sides" during the attack on the highway bridge at Orvieto.

There were the medals, too. In *Catch-22*, "men went mad and were rewarded with medals," often for deeds they never did. So too in Vietnam, where a Bronze Star was practically assured, especially to Saigon desk soldiers who had typewriters, and many of the medals, even though deserved, were awarded for fictional heroics because the actual sites of the events were not officially admitted to be in the war zone. Even today, many heroes cannot reveal that the citations on their truly deserved awards are invented. Similarly, and more paradoxical, is the fact of the missing names from the Vietnam War Memorial, names of those Americans killed in action while in combat against the VC [Viet Cong], North Vietnamese, or Pathet Lao before the "official" date of U.S. involvement in Vietnam. Any one of these men would have made a fitting tentmate for Yossarian, like "Mudd the unknown sol-

Airborne troops including both U.S. and ARVN soldiers leap from a helicopter as they prepare to move into a combat area in Vietnam. AP Images.

dier who had never had a chance." As was Mudd, these men are "really unknown" and should be recognized.

Scenes in *Catch-22* Prefigure Events in Vietnam

The parallels continue. Although few pilots were privy to the facts of the regular "Tuesday lunch" in Washington where all missions into North Vietnam were approved personally by the president, some of the fighter pilots' songs such as "Mañana" showed that someone, at least, understood:

> Before we fly a mission
>
> And everything's o.k.
>
> Mac[namara] has to get permission from
>
> Flight Leader LBJ [President Lyndon B. Johnson].

One is reminded of Clevinger's quivering rationalization. "But it's not for us to determine what targets must be destroyed or who's to destroy them. . . . There are men entrusted with winning the war who are in a much better position than we are to decide what targets have to be bombed." A major target in North Vietnam was, of course, the Thanh Hoa bridge, which was not destroyed until the last days of the war despite ingenious attempts such as Project "Carolina Moon" on May 30, 1966. A specially modified C-130 was to drop 5,000-pound "pancake" bombs about 8 feet in diameter. At night, at 400 feet and 150 knots, the C-130 delivered five bombs near the bridge, then returned to base despite heavy groundfire. The next day's reconnaissance revealed no sign of damage or exploded bombs. One wonders if Yossarian would have returned to the target that night, as another C-130 did "with only slight modification in its route of flight." This aircraft disappeared and was never heard from again. Yossarian made his second bombing run over the bridge on the river Po, and when asked why, he replies, "We'd have had to go back there again. . . . And maybe there would have been more losses, with the bridge still left standing."

Not only bridges but mountain passes too provide irony for both *Catch-22* and the Vietnam War. In *Catch-22* an attempt is made to interdict a road in order to block two armored divisions coming down from Austria. The plan is to destroy a small mountain village that "will certainly tumble right down and pile up on the road." Dunbar objects: "What the hell difference will it make? . . . It will only take them a couple of days to clear it." Colonel Korn refuses to listen. "We don't care about the roadblock," he says. "Colonel Cathcart wants to come out of this mission with a good, clean aerial photograph he won't be ashamed to send through channels." The hundreds of air force and navy pilots who flew missions against Vietnam's Mu Gia or Ban Karai passes may see some real truth here.

There are many more episodes in *Catch-22* that seemed to prefigure the facts of aerial combat in Vietnam, not the least of which is the question of the number of missions, the basis of the concept of the phrase "Catch-22" itself. To document the various Vietnam War mission requirements for awards and decorations and for rotation home would require a book-length computer printout; it is enough to say that some missions counted, others did not, depending upon the dates they were flown, the country to which they were directed, and the Rules of Engagement at the time. I often heard pilots say "Catch-22" when these rules were changed, but thanks to their understanding of Heller's concept, most of them accepted with grace what they knew was craziness. As one F-4 pilot put it:

> Flew on Dave Connett's wing on his final mission. It was a spectacular display for his finale. The night was moonless and we were using napalm and CBU's [cluster bombs] on a storage area. The above mission turned out to be my final one also. I completed 102 in all but, because of a ruling halfway through the tour, some of the missions into Laos didn't count after 1 February 1966.

Other events of note are the sad prefiguring of fragging in the plot to kill Colonel Cathcart, and the unpublicized, but severe infighting among and within the Central Intelligence Agency, State Department, and Department of Defense as well as among the services, as can be seen in General Peckem's plan to grab control of all commands. There is also the frightening rationality of Ex-PFC Wintergreen when we first meet him in the novel. He has no objection to digging holes at Lowry field "as long as there was a war going on." His reason: "It's a matter of duty, . . . and we each have our own to perform. My duty is to keep digging these holes, and I've been doing such a good job of it that I've just been recommended for the Good Conduct Medal. Your duty is to screw around in cadet school and hope the war ends before you get out." It is a recorded fact that candidates for admission to the service academies presented higher and higher test scores as the Vietnam War progressed, and that when the draft was rescinded in 1972, resignations of cadets suddenly increased. While teaching *Catch-22* during this period at the United States Air Force Academy, I heard many slightly embarrassed laughs from my draft-exempt students when I highlighted Wintergreen's credo. One cannot argue with reason—or with Ex-PFC Wintergreen, wherever he may be today.

It's quite apparent, then, that in both general and specific areas, *Catch-22* did indeed provide a paradigm for many aspects of the Vietnam War. And as those just starting in the military during the mid-1950s snidely called some commanders Captain Queeg [from Herman Wouk's *The Caine Mutiny*], so did the names Colonel Cathcart and Major Major pass often from the lips of the Vietnam-era military men. *Catch-22* as novel had influenced our thinking, but Vietnam as Catch-22 itself affected our immediate existence.

I believe, too, that knowing Heller's work, seeing such irony and paradox come alive, made many of us more able to cope with the unreal reality of Vietnam.

Catch-22 Uses the Military as a Microcosm of Society

Wayne Charles Miller

Wayne Charles Miller was professor of English at the University of Cincinnati and the author of several articles and books, including A Gathering of Ghetto Writers: Irish, Italian, Jewish, Black, and Puerto Rican.

In this selection, Wayne Charles Miller finds Yossarian, Heller's hero in Catch-22, *to be searching for meaning in a chaotic world. Yossarian instead discovers absurdity around him in the U.S. Army Air Corps, and Miller contends that Heller depicts Yossarian's experience as representative of living in American society. Heller is part of a tradition that uses the military to symbolize society and criticize its conventions. Miller argues that Heller goes beyond earlier war writers by satirizing the sentimentality of their works.*

Yossarian, the hero of Joseph Heller's *Catch-22*, has little confidence in the universe but he would like to make some sense out of it. In effect, the very structure of the novel itself, resembling Lawrence Sterne's *Tristram Shandy*, suggests a chaotic world in which the perceptive intellect must impose order to find survival. Like a host of other American heroes, Yossarian is the single and somewhat rebellious consciousness in search of order amidst chaos, sanity amidst insanity, the meaningful life amidst a host of meaningless ones. In the process, he inspects the United States Army Air Corps as it functioned during World War II, American society as it is embodied in the fighting unit, western world culture at large, and the

God that that culture claims for its own. Invariably, his conclusions rest in the discovery of the absurd: absurd men pursuing absurd prestige and power, absurd nations fighting wars for absurd reasons, an absurd Christianity that no longer has meaning, and an absurd God who turns out to be the ultimate bungling authority figure. But, of course, if a system of values and beliefs is to be so inspected, some basis for judgment must be established.

Heller Uses the Military to Show the Absurdity of Society

In *Catch-22*, Heller offers Yossarian and his ultimately achieved value system as such a basis. In the last analysis, he is a pleasure-seeking animal who finds commitments to causes involving death and destruction irrational, particularly when the few in power prosper from such death and destruction that the masses suffer. He wants to make love; eat and drink well; have sensible friends; and, perhaps, like Holden Caulfield [in J.D. Salinger's *Catcher in the Rye*], save another soul or two from absurdity. Most of all, he wants to stay alive as long as he can. Yossarian, along with his companion, Dunbar, constantly stresses the fact that this life is the only one he has. To give it away to a cause that does not benefit him directly is an expression of the absurdity he abhors. The concentration upon the pleasures and happiness of this life and the acceptance of the idea that there is no continuation of the ego into another existence are at the heart of Yossarian's fascination for what he regards as the sensibleness of life in Sweden:

> He would certainly have preferred Sweden, where the level of intelligence was high and where he could swim nude with beautiful girls with low, demurring voices and sire whole happy, undisciplined tribes of illegitimate Yossarians that the state would assist through parturition and launch into life without stigma. . . .

While Heller suggests that this utopia of pleasure and nonresponsibility may be out of reach, he also suggests that there is nothing in the western world tradition that makes sense to his hero. Finally, Yossarian has faith only in his own existence and hope only in a more rational life in another country: a country that he feels exists outside the mainstream of western world capitalism and Christianity. Just as the World War I writers rejected commitments to duty, honor, country, Heller rejects commitments to the various faiths of his culture. From almost every angle of approach, Yossarian questions why he should die for an economic system in which he reaps few benefits or for a religious tradition he thinks is meaningless. Although Heller does not state it as baldly as [American screenwriter and novelist] Dalton Trumbo, his hero resembles one of the "little men" who, throughout the history of the western world, have fought and died for faiths from which they gained nothing. After making love to the wife of Lieutenant Scheisskopf, Yossarian considers the source of much of the faith of the western world: the benevolent God of Christendom.

> "And don't tell me God works in mysterious ways," Yossarian continued, hurtling on over her objections. "There's nothing so mysterious about it. He's not working at all. He's playing. Or else He's forgotten all about us. That's the kind of God you people talk about—a country bumpkin, a clumsy, bungling, brainless, conceited, uncouth hayseed. Good God, how much reverence can you have for a Supreme Being who finds it necessary to include such phenomena as phlegm and tooth decay in His divine system of creation? What in the world was running through that warped, evil, scatalogical mind of His when He robbed old people of the power to control their bowel movements? Why in the world did He ever create pain?"

For the most part, Yossarian is surrounded by pain, the death and destruction of the western world at war, and it is clear that Heller uses the microcosm of an American fighting unit as the means of pointing out the absurdity of that world and its values. Yossarian learns, for instance, that the ultimate product of war is the soldier in white whom the men are discussing in the hospital. Helpless, emasculated, defeated, he is the direct descendant of Faulkner's [Lt. Donald] Mahon and Trumbo's Johnny [Joe Bonham in *Johnny Got His Gun*]. "An unrolled bandage with a hole in it," he appears twice in *Catch-22* and represents the pointless waste of warfare.

Heller Satirizes the Sentimentality of Earlier War Novels

In a sense, *Catch-22* sums up a tradition. It is the clearing in the woods, the meeting ground, for almost all the themes and ideas developed along the various paths followed by novelists dealing with Americans at war and Americans within the military structure. Like [Herman] Melville, the first in the tradition to use the military world as a microcosm of a larger social order, Heller uses the base at Pianosa as a mirror of the culture of the United States. Like Melville and [Stephen] Crane, he presents his hero in danger of being emasculated in the totalitarian system: without recourse to justice and unable to assert his individuality within the corporate or command structure. Like [writer John William] De Forest, he is critical of professional officers, viewing them as men in love with warfare and its results: death, destruction, pay and promotion. Like most of the World War I novelists and some from World War II, he uses his work as a vehicle for criticism of an entire culture. But, while he may condemn the concepts of honor, glory, and patriotism just as much as [Ernest] Hemingway and [John] Dos Passos, he does not follow along the path established by them. In fact, at several points, Heller seems to satirize the element of sentimentality in the war novels that precede his. Particularly noteworthy is his presentation of the relationship between Yossarian and Luciana, the beautiful Italian girl permanently scarred by an American bombing raid. In a situation in which Hemingway might have had the lovers attempt an escape to an idyllic life in the mountains, Heller merely debunks the entire concept of romantic love.

Although *Catch-22* contains most of the characteristics of the lengthy tradition, one must step outside its limited domain to find Heller's predecessor in terms of its ultimate world view. Clearly, his is not the spirit of the protesters of World War I: serious, concerned, and hopeful about change. Rather, he seems more like Mark Twain in *The Mysterious Stranger* or in some of the selections Janet Smith has gathered in *Mark Twain on the Damned Human Race*. Here it is, he tells the reader, in all its irrationality and hopelessness, announcing that man's capacity to laugh at it may be the only indication of his sanity. In short, Heller introduces a new element into a major novel in the tradition—the element of satire. He directs its thrust at everything in the culture that is destructive, death-dealing, or authoritarian—those things that the rational mind regards as irrational. In another context, just as Twain provided an escape for his most representative hero, Huck Finn, from an American society he satirizes in *Adventures of Huckleberry Finn*, so too, Heller provides escape for his hero from a culture which would destroy him. For Huck there was still the territory, the vast virgin land of hope that the continent provided. For Yossarian there is no territory of freedom in an already established America. For him there is Sweden and the hope for a more rational life. As a highly individualistic hero, he must flee an increasingly rigid and corporately structured America in order to pursue that individuality. . . .

Discovery of Truth Leads to Yossarian's Escape

In its structure, *Catch-22* builds toward a climax that represents Yossarian's discovery of the final truth concerning human existence. Mentioned at key points throughout the novel, the actual description of the discovery occasioned by Snowden's death appears in Chapter Forty-One—just before the catch-all of the concluding chapter in which Heller provides for his hero's escape. It is in this discovery of Snowden's last moments that Heller places the important final impetus in Yossarian's rejection of the culture and the people responsible for the young man's death. In his helplessness in the face of Snowden's agony, Yossarian learns the importance of life and the absurdity of commitments to abstract ideals of a religious or economic or political nature. . . .

The Hopefulness of the End Contradicts the Rest of *Catch-22*

In the closing pages of the book much of the caricature and satire disappear; at one point Heller has Danby voice the essential problem that a deserter in the war against fascism must face:

> "I mean it, Yossarian. This is not World War One. You must never forget that we're at war with aggressors who would not let either one of us live if they won."

> "I know that," Yossarian replied tersely, with a sudden surge of scowling annoyance. "Christ, Danby, I earned that medal I got, no matter what their reasons were for giving it to me. I've flown seventy goddamn combat missions. Don't talk to me about flying to save my country. I've been fighting all along to save my country. Now I'm going to fight a little to save myself. The country's not in danger any more, but I am."

> "The war's not over yet. The Germans are driving toward Antwerp."

> "The Germans will be beaten in a few months. And Japan will be beaten a few months after that. If I were to give up my life now, it wouldn't be for my country. It would be for Cathcart and Korn. So I'm turning my bombsight in for the duration. From now on I'm thinking only of me."

Heller hedges here on the universal issue of pacifism and conscientious objection, but he clearly approves of his hero's decision to strike out on his own and thus abandon the absurd structure of which he is a part. The note of optimism at the close of the novel rings false and is generally out of tune with the satirical savagery of most of it. Had Heller continued in a satirical vein, perhaps Yossarian would have kept his deal with Cathcart and Korn. As it is, from Chapter Thirty-Nine— "The Eternal City"—forward, the tone of the work changes radically. It seems evident that in the face of the horrors of the western-world past represented by Rome, the eternal city, and the affirmation of the savage present in Snowden's death, Heller wishes to express some hope in the future. By permitting Yossarian at least to attempt escape from the insane world of the United States Army Air Corps in the Mediterranean to the hope of a better world in Sweden, he moves from the tone of Twain's *The Mysterious Stranger* to the closing hopeful gesture of *Huckleberry Finn*. He also leaps out of the pessimism of such twentieth-century novelists of the military as Hemingway, Faulkner, and Dos Passos. Their inspectors of United States and western world values—in the military novels and in others—are almost exclusively caught and victimized by the culture. For Jake Barnes, Frederick Henry, Harry Morgan, Robert Jordan, Robert Cantwell, Donald Mahon, John Andrews [central characters in Ernest Hemingway's *The Sun Also Rises, A Farewell to Arms, To Move and Move Not, For Whom the Bell Tolls*, and *Across the River and into the Trees*, and in William Faulkner's *Soldier's Pain* and John Dos Passos's *Three Soldiers*, respectively], and others, there was no chance of escape. All end in death or defeat. In fact, Huck Finn's most obvious twentieth-century counterpart, Holden Caulfield, finds no place to escape in America except to a rest home. But, if Heller violates the tone of his work by returning to a nineteenth-century hopefulness about the young American hero, he has prepared the way for it within the context of

Catch-22 itself. For, while Yossarian is typically a twentieth-century American product insofar as he is from a large urban center, New York, and embodies some urban sophistication and skepticism, there exists in the novel a character who is as rural, as practical, and as alone as Huck himself. Combining the pragmatism of Huck with the individualism of a [Henry David] Thoreau, the inscrutable Orr looks as innocent as Alfred E. Neumann [the hero of *Mad* magazine] as he cunningly and quietly plans his escape from Pianosa to Sweden. When the chaplain brings word that Orr has landed his raft in Sweden and in so doing has restored the religious man's faith in God, Yossarian is ecstatic. The rural, simple, innocent American has shown him the way. . . .

With devastating satire, Heller deals with the potential military monks he finds at Pianosa, and it is clear that he intends them to be representative of American culture at large. In fact, until the change in tone that occurs in Chapter Thirty-Nine, the primary direction of the novel is toward the satirical destruction of an American life Heller clearly regards as immoral and absurd. Using the military unit as a microcosm, he takes on American business, education, medicine, organization men, and religion. Caught in the frenzy of a nation geared for war, Yossarian faces them all. . . .

Yossarian Rejects an Absurd Existence

To be a sane man in an insane environment means that one must be judged insane by the caretakers of that environment. In specifically American military terms, Yossarian inhabits a world in which justice has become a joke, in which money and profit mean more than lives, and in which religion and psychiatry are in the service of a unitary state. For it is clear that Yossarian's world at Pianosa is Heller's microcosm for life in the United States. He takes a more destructive view of that culture than any other American military novelist and pre-

sents it as an environment in which pyramid-climbing sharp-
ies and money-hungry entrepreneurs thrive and rule. . . .

Heller sees [men] becoming human defectives in [the military world]. Suggesting essentially the same idea concerning
the organization man that [John Horne] Burns voices in *The
Gallery*, he is careful to establish that almost all the successes
within the system are either completely sexless or at least incapable of love. For instance, Cathcart maintains a villa where
the men imagine he engages in orgiastic weekends in the
country. He cultivates that image but actually spends his time
there shooting birds. The most ominous success, and, in
Heller's view, the most typical of an identifiable military mentality, is Scheisskopf. Perfectly named [German for "shithead"],
he rises from Lieutenant to Colonel, and, surpassing Cathcart,
to General during his climb of the corporate pyramid. A military martinet, his monomaniacal desire is to have men march:
mechanically, uniformly, in step. As a lieutenant, he devises a
method by which his unit's marching will be better than any
of the other squadrons. In order to have their arms move in
unison, he wishes to have "a friend of his in the sheet metal
shop sink pegs of nickel alloy into each man's thighbones and
link them to the wrists by strands of copper wire with exactly
three inches of play. . . ." In the pursuit of such order, Scheisskopf neglects his wife; the training cadets do not. When she
informs her husband that she might be pregnant, he replies
that he does not have time for such nonsense: "'Don't you
know there's a parade going on?'" Later, when he needs a live
model and asks her to march for him, she asks hopefully if he
wishes her to march in the nude. "Lieutenant Scheisskopf
smacked his hands over his eyes in exasperation. It was the
despair of Lieutenant Scheisskopf's life to be chained to a
woman who was incapable of looking beyond her own dirty,
sexual desires to the titanic struggles for the unattainable in
which noble men could become heroically engaged": such as,
Heller implies, making men march. The last view that the

reader has of Scheisskopf reveals that he has attained the rank of general and has broadened his horizons as a result. He wants *everybody* to march.

Again, not Yossarian. As Heller completes his creation of a microcosm of a culture in which men are emasculated by their reliance upon authority and by their pursuit of wealth, prestige, and power, he increasingly moves his hero along a path of ultimate rejection of that culture. But it is not only the capitalist-Christian-authoritarian structure of the United States which Yossarian rejects. Heller sees in that society merely the inevitable and tragic repetition of the absurdity of European history: its warfare, its class structure, its monomaniacal pursuit of wealth; its childish reliance upon authority in matters of religion and politics. Yossarian, the individualistic rationalist, rejects it all.

In the critical chapter "The Eternal City," in which he becomes less like Candide [the optimistic young hero in the satire by Voltaire] and more like Hamlet [the melancholy hero of the Shakespearean play], Yossarian walks the streets of Rome, the city in *Catch-22* which becomes the symbolic source of western world culture. Reminiscent of Raskolnikov's [the protagonist of Fyodor Dostoyevsky's *Crime and Punishment* walks through the streets of St. Petersburg and his dream of Mikolka beating the horse to death because it is his private property, Yossarian inspects the horrible reality of a degraded human condition. As he walks, he views some of the representatives of massive poverty: "the shivering, stupefying misery in a world that never yet had provided enough heat and food and justice for all but an ingenious and unscrupulous handful." He sees men torturing other men and making jokes about it— everywhere the powerful or the many violating the meek or the good. Against the ancient fluted Corinthian columns of the Ministry of Public Affairs, he witnesses a group of soldiers raping an Italian girl. He sees men beating dogs and children, and he watches a mob of police brutalizing a man with an armful of books. As he walks, he thinks: "The night was filled with horrors, and he thought he knew how Christ must have felt as he walked through the world, like a psychiatrist through a ward full of nuts, like a victim through a prison full of thieves." A monk, obviously suggesting both the ineffectuality and the irresponsibility and guilt of the Church and Christendom, walks with his head down and notices nothing. When Yossarian arrives at his destination, the apartment for the officers from his Group at Pianosa, he discovers that Aarfy, in many ways a typical American boy who is anxious to pursue success in a corporate structure, has raped and killed the helpless, simple, ugly, and innocent maid whom the men had always left alone.

It is the face of this past that Yossarian rebels against its ultimate product in the present—the corporately constructed war machine of the western world. After his discovery in Rome he absolutely refuses to fly any more bombing runs in a war that makes money for the Minderbinders and Daneekas and provides status and prestige for the Scheisskopfs and Carthcarts. In so doing, he becomes a threat to the system of corporate control. Heller sums up the situation: "Morale was deteriorating and it was all Yossarian's fault. The country was in peril; he was jeopardizing his traditional rights of freedom and independence by daring to exercise them." But at this point Yossarian is neither a Quixote [hero of Miguel de Cervantes' *Don Quixote*, a parody of chivalry and idealism] nor an Orr. Interested in his own happiness and comforts, he agrees to the deal proffered by Cathcart and Korn. If he will keep quiet and not spread his dissent to the other members of the bomb group, they will send him home as a hero. Call me Blackie, says Korn; call me Yo Yo says Yossarian. In making the deal, Yossarian follows the dictates of the cynical old man who sits in the direct center of the garish and pathetic whorehouse which the men frequent. By defeating every argument that the idealistic but misguided American boy, Nately, could offer, it seems the old man gains ultimate victory. Indeed, within the context of their conversation, Nately had seemed absurd when he shouted that anything worth living for was worth dying for. But, absurd or not, the spirit of that kind of idealism lives on in Yossarian, and a series of events prevents him from accepting Cathcart and Korn's arrangement.

First of all, Nately's whore, performing the function of *deus ex machina* [a contrived and too-easy resolution of a problem in a story], turns on the traitor as he leaves Cathcart's office, and stabs him several times.

> Yossarian thought he knew why Nately's whore held him responsible for Nately's death and wanted to kill him. Why the hell shouldn't she? It was a man's world, and she and everyone younger had every right to blame him and everyone older for every unnatural tragedy that befell them; just as she, even in her grief, was to blame for every man-made misery that landed on her kid sister and on all other children behind her. Someone had to do something sometime. Every victim was a culprit, every culprit a victim, and somebody had to stand up sometime to try to break the lousy chain of inherited habit that was imperilling them all.

Then, the helplessness he feels at the hands of the operating doctors suggests the helplessness of the individual once under the anesthesia of complicity in the system. Finally, the news of Hungry Joe's death and the remembrance of the lesson Snowden taught him seal Yossarian's fate. He cannot become a part of an organizational structure whose last resort of control is Catch-22, the catch that suggests that the use of power is the answer to all questions and that one must always obey one's superiors regardless of what their orders are.

Not a Typical War Novel

Because of the satirical tone throughout most of the novel, *Catch-22* is by no means a typical example of the American military novel. Nor is it even representative of most of the fiction that emerges from World War II. Published sixteen years after the close of the war, the book is more about the United States in the postwar era than about the conflict itself. It is clear, for instance, that Captain Black's Glorious Loyalty Oath Crusade is direct satire upon McCarthyism and the anti-Communist hysteria he [Sen. Joseph McCarthy] bred. And Heller is surely satirizing the military-industrial complex that grew during the fifties when he has Major Danby comment on the relationship between Minderbinder and Cathcart: "'Milo and Colonel Cathcart are pals now. He made Colonel Cathcart a vice-president and promised him an important job after the war.'" In a larger context, *Catch-22* is concerned with the general direction the country has taken since 1945. . . . Snowden taught Yossarian that "The spirit gone, man is garbage." Heller in *Catch-22*, takes his readers on an inspection tour of a world in which the spirit of individualism and freedom has been drained from its members in the name of security and obedience. If one is to survive, then, in General Cummings' words, one must learn to fit into a "ladder of fear."

Since Yossarian is a representative of the traditional questing spirit of the liberal American, it is perhaps Heller's statement of ultimate hopelessness that his hero must seek rationality in another country and in another sociopolitical framework. While it is true that the change in tone near the close of the novel provides hope for the hero, his symbolic dismissal of the United States indicates a complete denial of the values of that culture for, if [Samuel] Huntington is correct and the nation is moving toward the kind of authoritarianism Melville envisioned in *White Jacket*, then the hero representative of a liberal optimism must disappear. Perhaps the fact that Heller uses such a figure, Yossarian, for most of *Catch-22* as a device to satirically expose the culture is the first step toward a situation in which the liberal American hero will go underground. It seems less alarmist, however, to suggest that Yossarian will not be the last of those idealistic heroes whose discovery of the realities of American and western world values leads them either to escape or to cynical acceptance. Even in the character of Colonel Ross in [James Gould Cozzens'] *Guard of Honor* one senses even the "adjusted" man's disappointment with what seems to be his conception of ultimate knowledge: that it is for children to concern themselves with absolutes and that the mature man finally must concern himself with processes and with the ultimate problem of keeping an organization or a culture afloat. In fact, Cozzens' world in *Guard of Honor* is somewhat similar to Heller's in *Catch-22*. In both, men are destructive, insensitive, self-seeking, and for the most part unconcerned with any transcendent cultural values. Certainly, Mowbray's arrangement of a party for a General which results in wholesale death is as gruesome as Cathcart's constant volunteering of his men for more missions or Scheisskopf's desire to make his charges march. Both books are ultimately concerned with a social structure which dwarfs its members and controls their lives. Cozzens, with some resignation, announces that, after all, this is the way it is; Heller, despite the bitterness of his view of the culture, holds out hope in the transcendent figure of Yossarian. It remains an open question whether this affirmation, involving as it does, a complete shift of tone in the novel, is merely a device enabling Heller to avoid an ultimate blackness which is totally destructive. Although he may recognize that Sweden represents only another illusion, his final statement in *Catch-22* may be the insistence that such illusions and such ideals are the means by which men and cultures survive.

Catch-22 Is About Being Endangered by One's Own Government

Seth Kupferberg and Greg Lawless

Seth Kupferberg and Greg Lawless were editors of the Harvard Crimson *while at Harvard in the mid-seventies. Lawless is also the author of* The Harvard Crimson Anthology: 100 Years at Harvard.

In this interview with the editors of the Harvard Crimson, *Heller says that the perversity of the military in* Catch-22 *really was not characteristic of the military in World War II. He notes, however, that it was characteristic of the military in the Korean War, the Cold War, and the Vietnam War. He set* Catch-22 *during World War II only because he knew that war. Heller goes on to say that the real danger to the citizenry is from the government.*

Seth Kupferberg and Greg Lawless: Christopher Lehmann-Haupt *in his* New York Times *review the other day said that* Something Happened *would anticipate the seventies just as* Catch-22 *anticipated the rise of the military-industrial complex in the sixties. Do you believe that?*

Joseph Heller: No. *Catch-22* was written, not before you were born, but it was partly in outline before you were born. It was published in '61. And in '61 ... ah ... Kennedy was president. ... It *did* anticipate—in the sense that it came before the Vietnam war—everything the Vietnam war brought with it, which was—it's not a phrase that I ever use—the 'military-industrial complex.' But it was there and certainly it grew with the whole morality of deception practiced by the executive in dealing with the American people and other nations, which often involves lying and distortion. But what I have to say about the military in *Catch-22*: I don't recall it being characteristic of the military in World War II. It was characteristic of the military during the Korean War, during the Cold War, and became manifest during the Vietnam War. It was just a perversion of all codes of honor that are being taught at Annapolis or in American military justice. Misuse of the FBI, the CIA, misuse of the courts, the attorney-general's office, and so forth. Political persecutions. Indictments would be started, trials would be carried out even though the chances of conviction were non-existent, or if convictions were achieved reversal was a certainty afterwards—I'm referring to the [pediatrician Benjamin] Spock trial, or the [military analyst Daniel] Ellsberg trial, the Ellsberg trial was a continuation of these things. All these cases are political. We all know that the Ellsberg trial was an attempt by the White House to discredit Ellsberg, or else to persecute him whether they got a conviction or not. Tying somebody up in a trial for two or three years is punishment, and it's a very great punishment. As I say, I don't recall *Catch-22* being characteristic, it *wasn't* characteristic of the military in World War II.

Why did you set the novel in World War II?

Because I know World War II. I set it toward the end of World War II, the last few months, when Germany was not a factor. The dangers of *Catch-22* don't come from the enemy— they do as far as the flak goes—but the real dangers are the ones that continue after the war comes to an end. Yossarian's own superiors and their superiors are no different from the enemy. All right, *Catch-22* is about a person being destroyed by the war, . . . from their own superiors from within the organizations of which they are a part. That is the truth of this country.

What did Yossarian do after he took off?

I don't know. And I don't think that's really a bona fide question to ask about a book. My book ends with him taking off . . . ah . . . and I can live with the thing like that. I don't know about the reading public. I leave with him getting out of the hospital without being either captured or stabbed by Nately's whore.

But supposing he got to Sweden?

That becomes a different book . . .

What would he do when he got there?

He doesn't expect to get to Sweden, he makes that—I make that—clear. He hopes to get to Rome and take his chances from there. What does he do when he gets there? That's not part of the book. He would probably have to go underground as a fugitive . . . wait for amnesty . . . or be captured and punished. As long as he's free, he's free. I saw his being free as perhaps inspiring in others a more critical attitude, an attitude of inspection.

Catch-22 Is a Transitional War Novel

Joseph J. Waldmeir

Joseph J. Waldmeir is emeritus professor of English at Michigan State University and the author of numerous articles and books on American writers, including The Critical Response to Truman Capote. *With Adam J. Sorkin, he authored* Conversations with Joseph Heller.

In the following selection, Joseph J. Waldmeir declares Catch-22 *an important war novel because it is the only novel to treat World War II as absurd. In this sense, it is a transitional novel acting as a bridge between the realistic novels depicting the horrors of a necessary war and the postwar novels of a chaotic world. Waldmeir argues that* Catch-22 *ultimately fails in its portrayal of absurdity due to its chaotic structure. He also finds the scene where Yossarian declares his support for the war at odds with the antiwar sentiments of the rest of the book. Despite these flaws, Waldmeir finds some genuinely comic episodes in* Catch-22.

Joseph Heller's *Catch-22* . . . is the one [World War II] novel which attempts to treat the war as absurd. It proceeds from Heller's discovery that everything in the modern world is up for grabs; that nothing—and therefore, ipso facto, everything—makes coherent, logical sense. By the ancient comic device of portraying the preposterous as normal, it is possible to make of this discovery something delightfully, often uproariously funny, and Heller is superb at the creation of this kind of comedy.

Joseph J. Waldmeir, "Conclusion," in *American Novels of the Second World War*, Berlin: Mouton & Co., 1968, pp. 157–65. Copyright © 1968 in the Netherlands, Mouton & Co, N.V., Publishers, The Hague. Reproduced by permission of Mouton de Gruyter, a division of Walter de Gruyter & Co.

Catch-22 Treats War as Absurd

Nearly everything and everybody in *Catch-22* is outlandish, wacky. There is Lt. Scheisskopf whose monomaniacal love for dress parades finally earns him promotion to General. There is ex-PFC Wintergreen who, for all practical purposes, runs the war from his clerk's desk by manipulating orders and memoranda. There is the Major named Major Major Major who got his rank through an understandable IBM error, who doesn't want the rank nor know how to use it, and who consequently flees his office through a window whenever he is about to be approached with a problem. And there are others, equally wacky, but in a far more vicious, deadly sense: There is Captain Black who, out of jealousy of Major Major, institutes the Glorious Loyalty Oath Crusade in order to prove that Major Major is a Communist by the simple device of refusing to let him sign the Oath ("'You never heard him denying it until we began accusing him, did you?'"). There is Col. Cathcart who is most upset to learn that enlisted men pray to the same God as officers (recall the famous Mauldin cartoon of the sunset?) and that God listens to them; whose one great dream is to be immortalized in a feature story in the *Saturday Evening Post*, and who, to achieve this end, keeps raising the number of missions his squadron must fly until he has tripled the required number. There is Cpl. Whitcomb, the Chaplain's assistant, who devises a form letter to take care of the growing casualties resulting from Col. Cathcart's policy; the letter reads in part: "Dear Mrs., Mr., Miss, or Mr. and Mrs.: Words cannot express the deep personal grief I experienced when your husband, son, father, or brother was killed, wounded, or reported missing in action." And finally—though there are many others who could and some readers would argue should be mentioned—there is Milo Minderbinder, angle-shooter extraordinary, caricature of the American businessman. He forms a syndicate, M&M Enterprises, dealing in everything imaginable from Lebanese cedar to Dutch tulips, Swiss cheeses, Spanish oranges, and Egyptian cotton. He insists that he operates a legitimate business in the American way, for each member of the squadron is a shareholder in the syndicate; and, since business is above quarrels between nations, there are English, French, German, and Italian partners in the syndicate as well—all of which makes very little difference since the profits are all plowed back into the business anyway, and there are no holds to share. Milo sells petroleum and ball bearings to the Germans and even contracts with them, in a major coup for the syndicate, to bomb and strafe his own airfield with planes of its own squadron. And because he is successful in the American tradition—that is, because his books show a substantial profit—Milo is admired and respected by the American people: even, though somewhat grudgingly, by those who lost loved ones in the bombing and strafing.

Lt. John Yossarian, a bomber pilot from whose point of view we observe most of the action, is one of the few even moderately "normal" characters in the novel. The others—the Chaplain, Doc Daneeka, Major Danby, each a friend and confidant of Yossarian—are all caught up to some degree in the prevailing absurdity. But Yossarian is not. Each of his actions, preposterous, indeed crazy though it might be, is carefully calculated both to protest the absurdity and to get him out of combat if not clean out of the service. He complains of a non-existent liver pain in order to be hospitalized to await the pains becoming jaundice so that it can be treated (the first variation of the elaborate joke upon which the novel is built: the doctors can cure jaundice, but a simple pain in the liver they cannot cure, whether the pain exists or not). He censors enlisted men's mail by editing the letters unmercifully, sometimes deleting all modifiers and articles, sometimes blacking out all but the salutation and close; and he signs as the name of the censoring officer either Washington Irving or Irving Washington. He either goes to sleep or behaves boorishly at briefing sessions. On the day that he is to be awarded a medal he appears in ranks totally nude, protesting that his uniform is covered with the blood of the man whose death earned him the medal. But his counter absurdity campaign is fruitless, the world being what it is. In the first place, Yossarian is not considered crazy by his superiors but simply insubordinate, and therefore eligible not for a Section-8, but for flying more combat missions. In the second place, there is the magnificently absurd logic of Catch-22 "which specified that a concern for one's own safety in the face of dangers that were real and immediate was the process of a rational mind". All one must do to be grounded for mental reasons, Doc Daneeka explains to Yossarian, is to ask; but asking is proof that one is not crazy. Put in another way: "If he flew [more missions] he was crazy and didn't have to; but if he didn't want to he was sane and had to."

The Novel Is Repetitive

The novel moves by fits and starts toward Yossarian's eventual desertion, but this is not a forward movement. It really does not go anywhere that it has not already been in its first few pages, albeit with slight variations in situation and character. In addition, there is no clearly juxtapositional relationship among its episodes; they are by and large interchangeable—so much so that many of them could actually be removed without marring the novel structurally at all. In fact, since Heller tends to tell the same joke and laugh the same ironic laugh over and over again, the removal of some of the episodes could cut down the repetitiveness, the redundancy, and improve the novel considerably. Plotless really, the book is unified by the pattern of absurdity established at its outset. But this is a tenuous unity at best; and it is here, faced with chaotic structure and endless repetition of episodes which individually are often quite funny, that one begins to feel doubt and dissatisfaction about the novel. Somehow, one feels, it would have been better if it had been better made.

In one sense, this criticism may seem rather picayune: after all, the novel remains brilliantly comic, episodic or not. But in another, higher sense, the criticism is of major seriousness, for the episodic flaw is symptomatic of the novel's failure—and most importantly, of its failure on its own terms: as absurd. Perhaps paradoxically, the successful portrayal of absurdity, because it requires a tightness rather than a looseness of form, also requires argument, the positing of directions from which and toward which and around which the action and the characters may move—requires if you will at least the potential existence of the Court or the Castle [as in Kafka's works] or Godot [as in Beckett's play] or the rhinoceros [as in Ionesco's play] or an American Dream [as in Miller's *Death of a Salesman*]. The artist must have a position, a point of view, some awareness of what things should or could be in order to be aware of the absurdity of things as they are.

Heller either lacks this awareness, or he prefers to focus upon the merely comic which is the inherent quality of the absurd. Milo Minderbinder is a case in point. This soldier-businessman who profits so heavily from the non-sense of war could have been made to crystallize war's absurdity, but he remains little more than a slapstick caricature whose exploits are too preposterous and overdrawn and directionless to be much more than burlesque blackouts. . . .

Catch-22's Ending Comes as a Shock

What *Catch-22* appears to be then is a not-too-serious anti-war novel—and serious or not, as such it would be a unique phenomenon within the literature of World War II. But appearances are deceptive; in this case, they apparently even deceived Heller. For in the final pages of the novel, he invests Yossarian with a totally unexpected idealism. In a scene between Yossarian and his friend Major Danby—a scene recognized even by Robert Brustein in his extremely favorable review as "an inspirational sequence which is the weakest thing in the book"—Yossarian justifies his imminent desertion against an appeal to his patriotism and his anti-Nazi conscience. "'This is not World War One'", Danby says. "'You must never forget that we're at war with aggressors who would not let either one of us live if they won.'" "'I know that'", Yossarian replies. "'Christ, Danby, I earned that medal I got, no matter what their reasons were for giving it to me. I've flown seventy goddam combat missions. Don't talk to me about fighting to save my country. I've been fighting all along to save my country. . . . The Germans will be beaten in a few months. And Japan will be beaten a few months after that. If I were to give up my life now, it wouldn't be for my country.'"

The scene comes as a shocking surprise. It represents a reversal of intention almost as flagrant as Wouk's in *The Caine Mutiny*. There is nothing wrong with an American novelist being in favor of the war; Heller would in fact, as suggested above, be unique if he opposed it. But since he appears to be opposed to it throughout the novel, there is something wrong with Yossarian, his victim-spokesman, expressing pro-war sentiments, weak and unconvincing though they might be. One might forgive the sequence if he could see it as even moderately integral, if the novel had prepared the way for it. But such is not the case; the sequence is not added up to, it is simply added on. Heller retreats from the seriousness of both social criticism and absurdity for 435 pages and then, as if in afterthought, seems to say: 'You see? This has all been a joke— good, clean fun with overtones of the macabre to titillate. But underneath, there has really been something deep and important going on.' Unfortunately however, there hasn't been.

[*Catch-22*] is a transition piece, looking backward to the war novels which portrayed war as barbaric but argued that this war was necessary, and forward to those post-war disaffiliates who portrayed the chaos of a world without convictions and values, and laughed at it. The novel's weakness grows out of Heller's inability to make up his mind whether he is an ideological war novelist, an anti-war novelist, or an *avant-garde* absurdist. But for our purposes, that weakness is a virtue for it helps us to comprehend once more most clearly the intellectual and emotional soul-searching which preceded the ideological novelists' commitment to the crusade, and to understand finally and fully the strength of that commitment.

Catch-22 Nearly Succeeds in Reflecting the Insanity of American Life

Norman Podhoretz

Norman Podhoretz is a literary critic and neoconservative political writer. He is the former editor in chief of Commentary *magazine and is the author of numerous articles and books, including his autobiography,* Breaking Ranks: A Political Memoir. *He was awarded the Presidential Medal of Freedom by President George W. Bush.*

In the following selection, Norman Podhoretz cites several notorious figures of the mid-twentieth century to prove his thesis that Catch-22 *accurately reflects the insanity of American life at that point in history. He suggests that* Catch-22 *would have been a better book without its ending; that is, if Heller had continued the earlier theme of the book that there is nothing on earth worth dying for.*

Not long ago, in an article in *Commentary*, [novelist] Philip Roth complained that the world we live in "is a kind of embarrassment to one's own meager imagination" as a novelist. "The actuality," Roth went on to say, "is continually outdoing our talents, and the culture tosses up figures almost daily that are the envy of any novelist. Who, for example, could have invented Charles Van Doren [the Columbia University professor who cheated on the 1950s TV quiz show *Twenty-one*]? Roy Cohn and David Schine [chief counsel and special consultant in the anti-Communist Army-McCarthy Hearings in 1954]? Sherman Adams and Bernard Goldfine? [President

Norman Podhoretz, "The Best Catch There Is," in *Doings and Undoings: The Fifties and After in American Writing*, New York: Farrar, Straus & Giroux, 1964, pp. 228–35. Copyright © 1953, 1954, 1955, 1956, 1957, 1958, 1959, 1962, 1963, 1964 by Norman Podhoretz. Reproduced by permission of author.

Dwight Eisenhower's chief of staff and the Boston textile executive he was accused of accepting gifts from] Dwight David Eisenhower [Five-star general and thirty-fourth president of the United States]?" Anyone who follows the daily newspapers or watches television with some regularity will understand what Roth is getting at. We do often seem to be inhabiting a gigantic insane asylum, a world that, as Roth puts it, alternately stupefies, sickens, and infuriates. No wonder the American writer has so much difficulty "in trying to understand, and then describe, and then make *credible* much of the American reality."

Catch-22 Makes Credible the Incredible Reality of Mid-Twentieth-Century Life

I think Roth's observation goes far toward explaining why Joseph Heller's *Catch-22* has provoked more enthusiasm than any first novel in years. Though ostensibly about an air force squadron in the Second World War, *Catch-22* is actually one of the bravest and most nearly successful attempts we have yet had to describe and make credible the incredible reality of American life in the middle of the 20th century. To describe and make credible; not, however, to *understand*; the secret of Mr. Heller's success lies precisely in his discovery that any effort to understand the incredible is bound to frustrate the attempt to describe it for what it really is. The way to portray insanity, in other words, is to show what insanity looks like, not to explain how it came about.

To be sure, Mr. Heller is a very good writer, with an exceptionally rich talent for comedy (both high and low) and a vitality of spirit that is nothing short of libidinal in its force. But I doubt whether even those virtues would have been enough to produce *Catch-22*; what was needed was the heroic power to resist all the temptations to understanding (or, if you like, sympathy) that must have arisen during the eight years it took to write this novel. I use the word "heroic" here without irony, for I can imagine that Mr. Heller was continually plagued by the fear that if he did not bow more deeply in the direction of simple plausibility, no one would find his story credible, and his characters and the fantastic situations he was putting them through would be understood as comic exaggerations rather than as descriptions of what the world actually does look like to a rational man. Who could have invented Charles Van Doren or Dwight David Eisenhower? Not, surely, a conventional painter of portraits, perhaps not even a great conventional painter of portraits. But [Charles] Dickens could have invented them—only in this case he would not have been caricaturing (if in fact he was ever caricaturing); he would have been performing an act of photography. So too with Mr. Heller, whose gift for caricature has made it possible for him to achieve a very credible description indeed of the incredible reality around us.

Yossarian's Paranoia Is a Sensible Response

The hero of *Catch-22* is a bombardier named Yossarian who is convinced that everyone is trying to kill him. This idea makes various people angry, especially his friend Clevinger. Clevinger is a man who believes passionately in many principles and who is also a great patriot. . . .

"No one's trying to kill you," Clevinger cried.

"Then why are they shooting at me?" Yossarian asked.

"They're shooting at *everyone*," Clevinger answered. "They're trying to kill everyone."

"And what difference does that make?"

Clevinger is certain that Yossarian is crazy. Yossarian, for his part, has not the slightest doubt that Clevinger is crazy. . . . In fact, everyone is crazy who thinks that any sense can be made out of getting killed. When Yossarian is told that people are

A scene from the 1970 film adaptation of Catch-22. The Kobal Collection. Reproduced by permission.

dying for their country, he retorts that as far as he can see the only reason he has to fly more combat missions is that his commanding officer, Colonel Cathcart, wants to become a general. Colonel Cathcart is therefore his enemy. So is the German gunner shooting at him while he drops his bombs. So is the Nurse in the hospital who doesn't like him, and so are countless others (including bus drivers all over the world) who want to do him in. He is in constant peril of his life. All men are, but no one seems to realize it as keenly as Yossarian and some of his friends—Dunbar, for example, who cultivates boredom because boredom makes time go slowly and there-fore lengthens his life. Everywhere, Yossarian reflects in con-templating the war, "men went mad and were rewarded with flying medals. Boys on every side of the bomb line were laying down their lives for what they had been told was their country, and no one seemed to mind, least of all the boys who were laying down their young lives." But Yossarian minds. He minds so powerfully that he can think of nothing else. After gorging himself on a marvelous meal one day, he wonders awhile if it isn't perhaps "all worth it." But not for long. The very next sentence reads: "But then he burped and remembered that they were trying to kill him, and he sprinted out of the mess hall wildly and ran looking for Doc Daneeka to have himself taken off combat duty and sent home."

Yossarian may mind about getting killed to the point of madness himself, but there is no question that we are meant to take his paranoia not as a disease but as a sensible response to real dangers. Colonel Cathcart, who keeps upping the number of combat missions the men in his command are required to fly before being sent home, is—just as Yossarian says—an idiot who cares only about becoming a general. General Dreedle and General Peckem and Colonel Cargill and Colonel Korn are all idiotic too, always engaged in ridiculous jurisdictional disputes and petty personal rivalries which are usually settled by the mail clerk at headquarters, ex-P.F.C. Wintergreen, through the simple expedient of forwarding one general's communications through channels and dropping the other's (whose prose Wintergreen considers too prolix) into the waste basket. There is also Milo Minderbinder, the mess officer, running a huge syndicate called M&M Enterprises in which the Germans too have a share (Milo even accepts a contract from the Germans to bomb his own outfit). Meanwhile, Yossarian has to go on bombing people he doesn't know, and men on the ground go on firing flak at Yossarian, whom *they* don't know. It is all very strange and bewildering.

The whole system is governed by Catch-22, which permits the authorities to do anything they please while pretending to a respect for the rights of the individual. Catch-22 contains many clauses. The most impressive we learn about early in the book, when the flight surgeon Doc Daneeka explains to Yossarian why he cannot ground a crazy man, despite the fact that the rules require him to ground anyone who is crazy. The catch is that the crazy man must ask to be grounded, but as soon as he asks he can no longer be considered crazy, since "a concern for one's own safety in the face of dangers that are real and immediate is the process of a rational mind." Yossarian is "moved very deeply by the absolute simplicity of this clause of Catch-22." So is Doc Daneeka, whose terror of death (and of being shipped to the Pacific where so many dread diseases can be contracted) is almost as great as Yossarian's and whose attitude toward the world is correspondingly similar: "Oh I'm not complaining. I know there's a war on. I know a lot of people are going to suffer for us to have to win. But why must I be one of them?"

Heller Ridicules the Idea That It Is Noble to Die for Your Country

What is the war in *Catch-22* all about? The only explanation anyone ever seems able to offer is that men are dying for their country and that it is a noble thing to give your life for your country. This idea Mr. Heller takes considerable pleasure in ridiculing. What does Colonel Cathcart's desire to become a general have to do with anyone's country? And what is a country anyway? "A country is a piece of land surrounded on all sides by boundaries, usually unnatural," an ancient Italian who has learned the arts of survival tells the nineteen-year-old Lieutenant Nately, "There are now fifty or sixty countries fighting in this war. Surely so many countries can't *all* be worth dying for." Nately is shocked by such cynicism and tries to argue, but the old man shakes his head wearily. "They are going to kill you if you don't watch out, and I can see now that you are not going to watch out." (This prophecy later comes true.) And in answer to Nately's declaration that "it's better to die on one's feet than to live on one's knees," the old man tells him that the saying makes more sense if it is turned around to read, "It is better to *live* on one's feet than die on one's knees."

The interesting thing is that there is scarcely a mention until the end of the novel of Nazism or fascism as an explanation of why the war may be worth fighting; if there were, Mr. Heller's point of view would have had a far greater degree of resistance to contend with than he actually allows it to encounter throughout most of the book. That he is aware of this problem is obvious from a dialogue between Yossarian and Major Danby (a "gentle, moral, middle-aged idealist") that takes place in the closing pages. Danby reminds Yossarian that the Cathcarts and the Peckems are not the whole story. "This is not World War One. You must never forget that we're at war with aggressors who would not let either one of us live if they won." Yossarian is provoked by this unanswerable argument into taking back everything he has previously stood for:

> I know that ... Christ, Danby ... I've flown seventy goddam combat missions. Don't talk to me about fighting to save my country. I've been fighting all along to save my country. Now I'm going to fight a little to save myself. The country's not in danger anymore, but I am. ... The Germans will be beaten in a few months. And Japan will be beaten a few months after that. If I were to give up my life now, it wouldn't be for my country. It would be for Cathcart and Korn. ... From now on I'm thinking only of me.

This statement comes as a surprise: one had supposed that Yossarian had been thinking only of himself all throughout the novel. If we take what this new Yossarian says seriously, then the whole novel is trivialized, for what we had all along thought to be a remorselessly uncompromising picture of the world written from the point of view of the idea that survival is the overriding value and that all else is pretense, lying, cant, and hypocrisy, now becomes nothing more than the story of a mismanaged outfit and an attack on the people who (as Yossarian puts it with a rhetoric not his own) always cash in "on every decent impulse and every human tragedy." No, the truth is that Mr. Heller is simply not prepared to go all the way with the idea that lies at the basis of his novel and that is the main tool he has used in making an incredible reality seem credible. He is simply not prepared to say that World War II was a fraud, having nothing whatever to do with ideals or values. I don't blame him for not being prepared to say that; it would not be a true thing to say. Yet for the purposes of this novel, it would have been better if he *were* prepared to say it, for in shrinking from the final ruthless implication of the premise on which *Catch-22* is built—the idea that nothing on earth is worth dying for—he weakens the shock of the whole book.

Are we then to conclude that Mr. Heller doesn't really mean what *Catch-22* so unmistakably seems to be communicating for most of its first four hundred pages? I think we must, for if he really meant it, it would not have been possible for him to end the book as he does, with Yossarian heroically refusing to seek his own advantage through cooperating with the Cathcarts and the Korns. (The ancient Italian who lectures Nately and who really does believe that survival is the only thing that counts would most certainly have accepted the opportunity that Yossarian turns down.) Nor, for that matter, would Mr. Heller have been capable of the gusto and exuberance which is *Catch-22*'s most attractive quality: the morality of survival is more likely to breed a quiet and weary irony than the kind of joyful energy that explodes all over the pages of this book.

Perhaps without quite knowing it, Mr. Heller has given us in Yossarian another brilliant example of a figure who first appeared in J.P. Donleavy's *The Ginger Man* a few years ago: the youthful idealist living in a world so insane that he can find nothing to which his idealism might genuinely attach itself, and who therefore devotes all his energies to exposing the pretenses of everything that claims to be worthy of his aspirations and his loyalty. He hungers desperately for something that might be worth laying down his life for, but since nothing is available and since he is above all an honest man, he tells himself that he has in effect chosen to live only for his own survival and that he had better not kid himself about it. But of course he *is* kidding himself—he is not capable of the ruthlessness and opportunistic cunning it takes to live such a life. Now that he has learned that preserving his honor means more to him than saving his skin, the only way out is to run off somewhere, to extricate himself from the insane and murderous world that has somehow grown up around him. And so Yossarian bolts and will try to make it to Sweden. Only—I find myself wanting to ask Mr. Heller—what will Yossarian come upon there, in that peacefully neutral place, that is worth dying for? After all, a life devoted to preserving the "self" is not so very different from a life devoted merely to staying alive, and you have just told us that Yossarian needs something bigger to attach his spirit to. So you see, there are more clauses in Catch-22 than even you knew about.

Yossarian's Escaping to Sweden Is an Ethical Decision

Alberto Cacicedo

Alberto Cacicedo is a professor of English at Albright College in Reading, Pennsylvahia, and the author of numerous articles on literature.

In this analysis of two novels about World War II, Catch-22 *and* Slaughterhouse-Five, *Alberto Cacicedo draws parallels with a famous movie from that war,* Casablanca. *Like Rick in* Casablanca, *Yossarian in* Catch-22 *is dealing with an event from the past too painful to remember and "too formative to leave behind." It is only when he recovers the memory of Snowden's death, Cacicedo states, that Yossarian can navigate his way to ethical action.*

A central issue that World War II raises for novelists is how to represent the ultimately inexpressible horrors of that war and, at the same time, engage the reader in a dialogue that might produce the *saeva indignatio* (savage indignation) that Jonathan Swift, for example, considered the affective preliminary to ethical social action. Scholars are convinced that Joseph Heller's *Catch-22* leads to such a vision of human responsibility issuing from indignation. As Robert Merrill puts it, "Yossarian deserts because he finally realizes there are greater horrors than physical pain and death." In Heller's own estimate, those greater horrors are "the guilt and responsibility for never intervening in the injustices he [Yossarian] knows exist everywhere." At the end of the novel, when Yossarian de-

Alberto Cacicedo, "'You Must Remember This': Trauma and Memory in *Catch-22* and *Slaughterhouse-Five*," *Critique*, vol. 46, no. 4, Summer 2005, pp. 357–61, 367. Copyright © 2005 by Helen Dwight Reid Educational Foundation. Reproduced with permission of the Helen Dwight Reid Educational Foundation, published by Heldref Publications, 1319 18th Street, NW, Washington, DC 20036-1802.

cides to go to Sweden, he does so specifically to run to his responsibilities: "Let the bastards thrive," says Yossarian, "since I can't do a thing to stop them but embarrass them by running away." In this case, the ethical decision is to estimate what one can credibly do to work against a mad, destructive system and then do it. . . .

The Effort to Recover Memory

Leaving aside specific points of disagreement, I concur with those critics who see in [Kurt] Vonnegut, as in Heller, an impulse toward ethical, responsible behavior. However, I argue that the central issue with which [*Catch-22* and *Slaughterhouse-Five*] concern themselves is not so much taking responsibility as getting to the point at which responsible action is possible. As I see it, to be ethical requires that one develop Swift's indignation against the injustices of the world and, in the context of these two novels, against the complacencies that lead to depravity and world war. To do that, one must squarely and unblinkingly face the memories of what one must fight against. As an instance of what I mean, consider the decisive moment in [the movie] *Casablanca*, when Rick is converted from a self-indulgent cynic to a loving, committed one. At that moment he asks Sam to play—not to play again, but just to play—"As Time Goes By," a song that for Rick opens the doors of memory on a past that had been too painful to remember consciously. As the flashback to that past transpires and Rick, along with the audience, revisits Paris on the verge of German occupation, it becomes increasingly clear that Rick's mutilated emotional life, which we have seen in the first part of the film, is a direct result of the pain of that past. The flashback makes us see that Rick's behavior in Casablanca has been poised delicately between leaving his love behind and still feeling his love as an affliction of the heart. I want to emphasize here that the particular circumstances of Rick's pain are romanticized and, ultimately, too sentimental to carry the burden of what I want to address in this paper. But I begin by referring to Rick's plight because in the refrain of Sam's song, "You must remember this," is the kernel of [psychiatrist Sigmund] Freud's double-edged insight into the effects of trauma on its victim. Rick's demand that Sam play the song and his effort finally to contend with a past too traumatic to recollect and yet too formative to leave behind is at the center of what I want to consider in regard to *Catch-22* and *Slaughterhouse-Five*.

These two novels make the effort to recover memory that is central to their narrative structures. In *Catch 22*, Yossarian's decision is ultimately, as he puts it, to stop "running away from my responsibilities. I'm running *to* them. There's nothing negative about running away to save my life." But that decision comes in the final chapter of the novel, specifically at a point in the narrative when Yossarian has finally remembered, clearly and with no ambiguities, the death of Snowden, the central traumatic event of his career as bombardier. Heller, in fact once said, "Snowden truly dies throughout *Catch-22*." That comment points to the fact that, throughout the entire novel, Yossarian's memory has worked its way around Snowden's death, giving the reader flashes of the event, sometimes as off-handed references but more often as grotesquely comical ones like the sudden eruption of the phrase, "Where are the Snowdens of yesteryear." But until the full revelation of the event in the next-to-last chapter, Snowden's death is never actually recollected or enacted in its full horror. To the extent that they puzzle the reader and make Yossarian seem bizarre beyond understanding, one result of those sometimes comical prefigurements of the horror is that they serve as "a kind of trap," as Merrill puts it, that makes the reader complicit in the carelessness of the General Dreedles and Colonel Cathcarts of this world. Then, when the horror becomes clear, the recurrence of the references to the event effects a conversion in which "we come to feel something like shame for our indiffer-

ence." Thus, the indignation that we felt at the horrors produced by self-interested officers turns inward and prompts in
us a desire to act against those horrors. It is, however, important to recognize that throughout the novel Yossarian is as
much in the dark as is the reader about the actuality of
Snowden's death. The novel circles around and around the
death precisely because Yossarian can neither remember it nor
forget it.

In that sense, Snowden's death is for Yossarian like Ilsa's
abandonment for Rick—although the implications of
Snowden's death are much more serious. David Seed has ana-
lyzed the lesson of Snowden's death, as finally recollected by
Yossarian. At that moment, as Seed reminds us, Yossarian
quotes Edgar's remark in *King Lear* "the ripeness is all." But
Seed points out that the circumstance of Snowden's death
"blocks off" the sense that the passage has in *Lear*, the attempt to induce a philosophical acceptance of death. On the
contrary,

> One important metaphysical theme of *Catch-22* is the physi-
> cal vulnerability of man. [...] Death in this novel is pre-
> sented as a conversion process whereby human beings be-
> come mere matter and are assimilated into the non-human.
> [...] Snowden [...] spills his guts, which happen to be full
> of ripe tomatoes, and so Heller implies that man may be-
> come no more than the fruit, vegetables and meat he con-
> sumes. Where Edgar pleads for acquiescence, however, Heller
> sets up Yossarian as a voice of refusal, of resistance to the
> inevitability of death.

As Merrill concludes, Snowden's secret is that "[i]t is the spirit
that counts, not 'matter'"—and Yossarian's acceptance of the
responsibility to stay alive is, in effect, a paradoxical affirmation of the spirit's capacity to transcend the limits of matter.
Thus, Yossarian's remembering becomes the impetus for the
ethical challenge that he takes up in the final chapter. In that
regard, it is worth noticing that in a book in which, for the

Alan Arkin as Captain John Yossarian and Art Garfunkel as Captain Nately in a scene from the 1970 film adaptation of Catch-22. © John Springer Collection/Corbis.

most part, the names of characters are the titles of chapters, not until Yossarian remembers Snowden's death is a chapter titled "Yossarian"—the final chapter in some sense, because Yossarian finally acts rather than reacts. . . .

Therapeutic Remembering of Trauma

Addressing the symptomatology of trauma in his book, *Beyond the Pleasure Principle*, Freud describes the case of a little boy who, traumatized by being abandoned by his mother, re-enacted the scene of the trauma over and over and over again. So striking was the event for Freud that it forced him to reconsider his original, relatively unproblematic idea of the pleasure principle, which had indicated that people who experienced traumatic events would avoid them or any object that might recollect the trauma. Working through the implications of the little boy's reenactments, Freud concluded that, for a child, such repetitions may reflect a self-conscious effort to

153

dominate the traumatic event, for, he said, children "can master a powerful impression far more thoroughly by being active than by merely experiencing it passively." But when the repetition is not a conscious reenactment of the traumatic event, the fact of repetition points toward neurosis. And, said Freud, the more powerful the trauma-precipitating event, the more likely that the conscious memory will be repressed as too dangerous for the psychic well-being of the individual, and the more likely that those repressed memories will express themselves in unconscious reenactments of the traumatic event.

Yossarian's behavior before recollecting Snowden's death and Vonnegut's behavior in trying to remember the bombing of Dresden duplicate the symptomatology of trauma that Freud described. The fictional character and the real novelist must revisit the traumatic event over and over again precisely because it has determined their lives in profound ways; yet, because of its horrific power, the event has also erased itself from their consciousness. The narrative structure of *Catch-22*, like that of Vonnegut's own life, is determined by vertiginous circlings around their respective central traumatic events. As James Mellard says of Yossarian, "[I]t is the protagonist's *moral* life, his *inner-life*, his *psychological* needs that account for the novel's delaying tactics." Once having achieved a clear memory, the result for the traumatized person is therapeutic in the sense that it enables him to confront the horror that he has endured and to act on that knowledge. . . .

In *Casablanca*, Rick puts [the idea that all of us are guest-observers of our own existences] in a compact way: the lives that he and Ilsa lead do not amount to a hill of beans. Even as he says that, because he has remembered, Rick is moving toward an ethical action that forces one to see that individual choice is much more than a hill of beans. Both *Catch-22* and *Slaughterhouse-Five* present the blockages, material and psychological, to ethical action that we all must navigate; but they also refuse to accent the idea that we are nothing but a hill of beans.

Social Issues
in Literature

Contemporary
Perspectives on War

The Iraq War Attracts Vietnam Veterans

Jonathan Finer

Jonathan Finer covered the Iraq War as a staff reporter for the Washington Post. He is currently a student at Yale University Law School.

In the following viewpoint, Jonathan Finer reports that dozens of Vietnam veterans have signed up for duty in Iraq, with the majority signing on as private contractors. Troubled by their negative experiences in Vietnam, these veterans want to correct the mistakes made during the earlier war, the author argues. Finer states that many Vietnam veterans believe that helping returning soldiers prepare for civilian life is one of the most valuable contributions they are making in Iraq.

As a young Marine officer leading patrols in Vietnam, John Holly swears he survived by knowing the tangled terrain better than his enemies did. As a private contractor in Iraq dealing with logistics and supplies, he now must navigate a bureaucracy he finds nearly as complex.

Maggie Godson sweated out the 1968 Tet Offensive at an Army firebase as a Red Cross worker sent to boost the morale of frontline troops. Almost 40 years later, the mother of two returned to war, reviewing transportation and facilities contracts in Baghdad.

Charles Thomas was wounded three times in Vietnam— the last time by a rifle shot that shattered his ankle as he stepped off a helicopter into an ambush—and limped home questioning whether U.S. soldiers should have been sent there in the first place. Now in Iraq, he says he is unequivocally proud of his mission.

"What I'm doing now's the kind of thing we should have done more of in Vietnam," said Thomas, 59, from North Potomac, [Maryland,] who manages development of Iraq's sewage and water systems. "The thing I regret most about my time [in Vietnam] was we were just plain fighters. We didn't go out and help people with their everyday lives."

Decades removed from the conflict that molded—and, for some, scarred—their generation, dozens of Vietnam veterans have signed up for duty in Iraq. Some are still in uniform, graying guardsmen and reservists activated as part of the largest call-up since the last time most saw combat more than 30 years ago.

But the majority have joined the legion of private contractors working on Iraq's reconstruction. Armed with boots-on-the-ground experience from a war many believe had devastating consequences for U.S. society, they say their goal is to ensure that Iraq, and the American soldiers fighting here, do not suffer a similar fate.

"We're all over here for pretty much one reason. There's a huge job to do, and we don't want anyone saying it didn't get done right," said Tommy Clarkson, who spent a year in Vietnam with the Army's 44th Signal Battalion and now works as a civilian spokesman in Baghdad for the Army Corps of Engineers.

In his nine months in Iraq, Clarkson has compiled a stack of manila folders, one for each of more than 70 Vietnam veterans he has met, 16 of whom came as soldiers.

Their Vietnam experiences run the gamut: infantrymen, fighter pilots, bridge builders, career counselors.

"Over here, people don't talk much about that stuff—it was a long time ago," said Clarkson, 62, whose wife, Patty, is also a contractor in Baghdad. "But you see a guy who looks like he could be one of these kids' fathers and you just know, so you ask him, 'Hey, were you over there?'"

Not all of them are guys. Godson, who has been married for 35 years and has two grown sons, came to Baghdad in 2004. She is working overseas for the first time since criss-crossing Vietnam by chopper with her fellow "Donut Dollies," named for the trailers full of pastries and coffee that volunteers traveled with in World War II. In Vietnam, their jungle attire consisted of blue seersucker dresses and black loafers.

"The guys were always happy to see us," said Godson, an energetic 62-year-old who grew up in Northeast Washington and went to high school and college in the District. She spent 25 years after the war working as a travel agent in South Carolina, but when her office was shuttered, she decided to return to the war zone. "It's different for soldiers now—with all the access to computers and phones, they don't have the same sort of isolation," she said. "But when we showed up in Vietnam, they didn't know what to make of us. It was like we were from another planet, and everyone wanted to talk to us."

Although there is no tally of how many Vietnam veterans have spent time in Iraq, there are probably barely a few thousand left in the active-duty military, according to Rick Weidman, director of government relations for the Vietnam Veterans of America. Many others serve in the National Guard and reserves.

Among the most striking differences between the two often-compared conflicts, according to those who have spent time both here and in Vietnam, is the fact that Iraq is under reconstruction while fighting still rages across much of the country. Another is the dearth of soldiers with experience in the 20th century's bloodiest wars.

"We used to have these World War II and Korea vets come around, and I would say, 'I am never going to be one of those old farts lecturing the kids about what it was like,'" said Holly, 59, a retired Marine colonel who did two frontline tours in

Lieutenant Colonel Bryan McCoy, commander of the 3rd Battalion, 4th Marines, on April 4, 2003, reflects on the death of one of his Marines in the battle around Al Kut in Iraq the day before. AP Images/Gary Knight/VII.

Vietnam, the second with an elite Force Reconnaissance unit. "Now I figure one of the most valuable things I can do is mentoring."

Holly came to Iraq in 2003 as the director for all non-construction logistical operations, such as supplying beds and medical supplies to hospitals and turbines to electrical plants.

The task he and the others face in helping rebuild Iraq is daunting. Thousands of projects have been completed or are underway. But reconstruction has been hobbled by an insurgency that proved deadlier than expected and by miscalculation of the degree of degradation of Iraq's infrastructure from years of neglect and the widespread looting that followed the U.S. invasion. U.S. funds allocated to the rebuilding effort are slated to be spent by the end of the year. And pressure is mounting in the United States for a substantial reduction in U.S. forces here.

"I volunteered because I thought I could help prevent another Vietnam," Holly said. "After we pulled out of there, we stuck our heads in the sand like an ostrich, said it was a mistake and we should never have gone. We basically forgot about the place. That would be the worst-case scenario here."

Their feelings about the Vietnam War represent nearly all sides in the long and unresolved public argument about the conflict. Thomas said that when he got out of the war and, soon after, out of the Army, he realized that he "had no idea why we went there in the first place. It just didn't make sense."

Holly, who graduated from the U.S. Naval Academy's storied Class of 1968, which included James Webb, the former Navy secretary and a noted novelist, and retired Marine Lt. Col. Oliver L. North, said some of the best evidence that the United States had not lost was that Vietnamese citizens now embrace American culture. "You go to Vietnam and they love Americans there," he said. "I was amazed by that."

Among their most valuable contributions to the current war effort, the veterans here said, is offering guidance on the readjustment to civilian life that lies ahead for younger soldiers. An estimated one in six service members in Iraq is expected to suffer from post-traumatic stress disorder, a psychological condition widely diagnosed among Vietnam-era veterans. Although the casualty rate for U.S. forces in Iraq is far lower than that at the peak of the Vietnam War, the myriad threats soldiers face here—including ever more deadly roadside bombs and suicide attacks—make the conflicts' psychological impact comparable, the veterans said.

"You never know who the enemy is unless you've got an electronic scoreboard that's changing all the time," Weidman said. "The Vietnam guys can help keep things light when they're in the field. Out there, humor can keep you alive. And they can explain that it will not be easy to leave Iraq behind and go back."

Army Master Sgt. Danny Huffman, 59, knows firsthand that while fighting a war is hard, coming home can be as great a challenge. In 1968, he returned as an alcoholic to tiny Yukon, Okla., after a tour as an artilleryman in Vietnam. Before turning his life around, he lost jobs and eventually his marriage to his high school sweetheart.

"I'd tell the younger guys to get help a lot quicker than I did," said Huffman, who said support networks of veterans helped pull him out of his funk. A reservist, he is on his second stint in Iraq as a finance officer for reconstruction projects in Baghdad, a dawn-to-dusk job with no days off.

"When I get home next time," Huffman said, "the hardest thing to get used to will be the eight-hour workdays. Over here, we're always raring to go."

The American People Share Responsibility for the Iraq War

Leonard Pitts Jr.

Leonard Pitts Jr. is a nationally syndicated columnist for the Miami Herald who won the Pulitzer Prize for Commentary in 2002. He is the author of Becoming Dad: Black Men and the Journey to Fatherhood.

While much has been written about the George W. Bush administration's responsibility for a war that should not have been fought in Iraq, Leonard Pitts Jr. claims in the following selection, written five years after the start of the war, that the American electorate is equally to blame. Despite the fact that the justification for the war—weapons of mass destruction—clearly did not exist, Bush was reelected. The lesson to be learned from this, Pitt argues, is that the American people should never again allow themselves to ignore uncomfortable truths.

A nd five years later [in 2008], here we are.

There were no weapons of mass destruction. We were not greeted as liberators. The war did not pay for itself. The smoking gun was not a mushroom cloud. There was no connection to 9/11. The course we stayed led over a cliff.

We Should Learn from the Iraq War

Worse, Iraq has become a recruiting station for Islamic terrorists. One presidential candidate foresees a 100-year occupation. Electricity is still a sometime thing in Baghdad. The war

Leonard Pitts Jr., "Iraq: 4,000 Americans, Innumerable Iraqis, $3 Trillion," *The Miami Herald*, March 19, 2008, p. A25. Copyright © 2008 Miami Herald. Republished with permission of Miami Herald, conveyed through Copyright Clearance Center, Inc.

that was supposed to pay for itself was recently projected to cost us $3 trillion—that's trillion, with a "t," that's a three followed by 12 zeroes, that's three million millions. And American forces have sustained more than 33,000 casualties, including 4,000 dead and 13,000 wounded too severely to return to action.

Pundits and politicians will spend a lot of time debating the war in Iraq on this, its fifth anniversary. They will analyze what we have achieved, pontificate on where we should go from here. I will leave those arguments to them.

Not that those are not worthy issues. But I cannot get beyond what is, for me, the one overriding truth of this war.

It should never have been fought.

Yes, I know: The point is moot. The war was fought, and there is nothing we can do about it. But I submit there is, in fact, at least one thing we must do. Learn from it.

Much has been made of the culpability of the Bush administration, of the arrogance and incompetence that midwifed this mess. Less has been made, however, of the culpability of Bush's accomplices, the enablers and facilitators who made this misadventure possible. By which I mean you and me, the American electorate.

Granted, many of us have been screaming No as loudly as we could from the very beginning or shortly thereafter. But many more refused to own what we knew, refused to accept the evidence of our own eyes and call this administration to account. We were scared beyond the ability to reason and wanted to feel safe, we were too heavily invested in lies to be turned aside by truth, we needed with a desperation to believe what we were being told, to buy what we were being sold.

Excuses. At some point, you have to stand up and be brave. Stand up like American women and men.

This, we have largely failed to do. Three months after the war began, when it was becoming clear there were no weapons of mass destruction, 56 percent of us told Gallup it didn't matter, said the invasion was justified regardless. Play that

Then President George W. Bush, Defense Secretary Donald Rumsfeld, Lieutenant General David Petraeus and Marine General Peter Pace meet at the White House on October 5, 2005 to talk to reporters about the status of Iraq's constitutional referendum approaches. AP Images.

back again: The primary rationale for the war was disintegrating like a sand castle in the waves, yet a majority of us shrugged and said, "Whatever." Like our president, we were impervious to truths we did not want to know.

That majority is a memory, but it lasted long past the point it should have, lasted long enough to enable this disaster, to send George W. Bush back to office claiming a mandate, to dig us in so deep the sun feels like a rumor, to create legions of new terrorists, to run up a bill that we will be paying off for generations, to take the lives of 4,000 Americans and Lord only knows how many Iraqis.

So yes, we should at the very least learn from this, commit it to communal memory, so that maybe next time a fear-mongering leader tries to stampede us into precipitate and unwise action, we will have the guts to stop and reason and own what we know. And to realize that the electorate has a role to play in the life of a free nation and it is not a mindless cheerleader.

One can only hope. In the meantime, here we are, five years later. The electorate has largely moved on, more concerned about the price of gas than the price of war.

But the war grinds on. Indeed, it has ground the president's approval rating down to the low 30s.

Maybe you think that's accountability at last. Me, I'm surprised it's still that high.

U.S. Government Policies Provoke Terrorism

Doug Bandow

Doug Bandow is a former special assistant to President Ronald Reagan and the Robert A. Taft Fellow at the Conservative Defense Alliance. He is the author and editor of several books, including Foreign Follies: America's New Global Empire.

In the following viewpoint, Doug Bandow urges American foreign policy makers to understand that actions have consequences. He claims that terrorist attacks are a direct result of U.S. intervention in the affairs of Middle Eastern countries, citing several examples from recent history to make his point. He concludes that the Iraq War has only become another terrorist cause.

Who said the following?

> There are a lot of things that are different now [after the invasion of Iraq], and one that has gone by almost unnoticed—but it's huge—is that by complete mutual agreement between the US and the Saudi government we can now remove almost all of our forces from Saudi Arabia. Their presence there over the last 12 years has been a source of enormous difficulty for a friendly government. It's been a huge recruiting device for al-Qaeda. In fact if you look at [al Qaeda leader Osama] bin Laden, one of his principle [*sic*] grievances was the presence of so-called crusader forces on the holy land, Mecca and Medina. I think just lifting that burden from the Saudis is itself going to open the door to other positive things.

Hint: it wasn't Rep. Ron Paul, the now famous outside presidential candidate who sparred with [2008 presidential

Doug Bandow, "War Without Consequence? Absurd," Ludwig von Mises Institute, May 22, 2007. Reproduced by permission.

contender and former New York City mayor] Rudy Giuliani [in a debate] over the impact of US foreign policy on terrorism. It was Deputy Defense Secretary Paul Wolfowitz in a May 2003 interview with Sam Tanenhaus of *Vanity Fair* magazine.

This neoconservative guru sounded suspiciously like Rep. Paul, who declared in the debate: "Have you ever read the reasons they attacked us? They attack us because we've been over there; we've been bombing Iraq for ten years. We've been in the Middle East." Paul then elaborated after Giuliani's rhetorical blast: "They don't come here to attack us because we're rich and we're free. They come and they attack us because we're over there. I mean, what would we think if we were—if other foreign countries were doing that to us?"

We all know, or like to think we know, what Americans would do. We would fight back.

Terrorists View America as Being at War with Them

By suggesting that Americans look at their own government's actions, Rep. Paul took a shot at one of the nation's biggest sacred cows: we can do whatever we want in the world without consequence. For decades that seemed to be true. But no longer. It is critical that we honestly and realistically assess the consequences of US foreign policy.

Doing so does not mean that Americans are "to blame" for terrorism. Or that the victims of 9/11 "deserved" what they got. Talking about the issue doesn't necessarily even mean that the United States should change what it is doing. But the first step to design good policy is to recognize the consequences—all of them, including the ugly, unexpected, and painful ones—of alternative strategies.

Unfortunately, the horror of 9/11 short-circuited the US political debate. It was hard for Americans to understand the murder of so many innocent people; the president and other politicians preferred to offer platitudes, claiming that Osama bin Laden & company hated us because we are so free—essentially, because we have a Bill of Rights. Some of the explanations didn't even make logical sense. For instance, President Bill Clinton once claimed that "Americans are targets of terrorism in part . . . because we stand united against terrorism."

The "they hate us because we are free" argument made no sense since these same terrorists ignored European and Asian countries which mirrored America's prosperity and liberty. Indeed, Osama Bin Laden dismissed the contention: "Contrary to Bush's claim that we hate freedom . . . why don't we strike Sweden?"

Moreover, terrorism did not start in New York City on that beautiful fall day in 2001. Terrorism is an old political tool, usually employed by non-state actors who lack police forces and militaries: left-wing anarchists used assassinations and bombings to destabilize Czarist Russia more than a century ago.

Terrorism was a particularly common tool of nationalist and communist groups in the latter 20th century. Palestinian terrorism against Israelis reflected this tragic, but common, history. Indeed, until Iraq, the most prolific suicide bombers were outside the Middle East—the Tamil Tigers in Sri Lanka.

All of these terrorists murdered, maimed, and destroyed to advance a political agenda. So do Islamists who attack the United States. Oddly, some American officials view Islamic jihadists as proto-communists or Nazis, "Islamo-fascists," whatever that means. (Terrorists are nasty people, but fascism as normally understood ain't their game.) Department of Homeland Security Secretary Michael Chertoff contends that Islamic extremists "aspire to dominate all countries. Their goal is a totalitarian, theocratic empire to be achieved by waging perpetual war on soldiers and civilians alike."

It's a fearsome sounding argument, but doesn't match the terrorism that we've faced. World domination is not on the lips of most actual jihadists—the murderers who committed bombings in New York City and in Jakarta, London, and Madrid, for example. There are no terrorist attacks against China. Assaults against Russia and India reflect much more mundane grievances: policy in Chechnya and Kashmir, respectively. Most of the world muddles along undisturbed by any terrorist attacks. It's a curious campaign for world domination.

In fact, the evidence is much stronger that, by and large, terrorists view an activist America as being at war with them. The point is not that their belief is true, or justifies slaughtering Americans. But dismissing their hatred as a result of our freedom ignores the ugly reality that endangers us.

Attacks Linked to U.S. Aggression

Paul Wolfowitz is not the only US official to understand this aspect of terrorism. In 1997 the Defense Science Board Summer Task Force on DoD [Department of Defense] Responses to Transnational Threats reported: "America's position in the world invites attack simply because of its presence. Historical data show a strong correlation between US involvement in international situations and an increase in terrorist attacks against the United States."

Moreover, many of the terrorists have explained why they have done what Americans find inexplicable—sacrifice their own lives to kill others. [Author and journalist] James Bamford records that Osama bin Laden and al-Qaeda's number two, Ayman al-Zawahiri, "believed that the United States and Israel had been waging war against Muslims for decades."

Why? Michael Scheuer, the anti-terrorist analyst at the CIA who authored *Imperial Hubris: Why the West Is Losing the War on Terror*, cites several American actions that offend many Muslims. The US military presence in Saudi Arabia, strong backing for Israel as it rules over millions of Palestinians, allied sanctions and military strikes against Iraq, and support for authoritarian Arab regimes. In fact, large majorities of Arabs and Muslims share these criticism of US policy, even as they express admiration for American values and products.

Supporting Scheuer's conclusion is the University of Chicago's Robert A. Pape. His research indicates that modern terrorist attacks confronted one form or another of foreign occupation. Paul Wolfowitz pointed to Saudi Arabia for a reason. After 9/11 most Saudi men professed their agreement with bin Laden about kicking out American military forces.

Some terrorist attacks could not be anything but retaliation for US intervention. Consider the 1983 bombing of the Marine Corps barracks in Lebanon. Was it because of American liberty? Or was it a plot to conquer the United States? No. The [Ronald] Reagan administration had foolishly intervened in the middle of a civil war to back the "national" government, which ruled little more than Beirut and was controlled by one of the "Christian" factions. Washington indicated its support by having US warships bombard Muslim villages.

Lebanese Muslims saw aggression, not liberty, and fought back with the only effective weapons that they had at the time. The point is not that Americans deserved to be attacked, but that they would not have been attacked but for being placed in the middle of a distant sectarian conflict. No wonder US policymakers prefer not to talk about the causes of terrorism.

Obviously, it's not always so easy to figure out why terrorists undertook a particular attack. But they commonly speak of taking revenge for American killings. And sometimes US officials unwittingly exacerbate the problem.

Sanctions against Saddam Hussein's Iraq were blamed for the deaths of 500,000 Iraqi children. The number is suspect and the ultimate culprit was Hussein, but the toll was significant. Yet when asked about these incontrovertibly innocent victims, Bill Clinton's U.N. Ambassador, Madeleine Albright, told *60 Minutes*: "we think the price is worth it." The image of US policy-makers callously writing off Muslim babies does not do justice to America, but it was the image projected by Albright throughout the Islamic world.

In his October 2004 video Bin Laden spoke of viewing dead Arab Muslims, after which "it entered my mind that we should punish the oppressor in kind—and that we should destroy the towers in America in order that they taste some of what we tasted, and so that they be deterred from killing our women and children." Bin Laden is evil, but he has a political objective, one that is inextricably tied to interventionist US policies.

Iraq War Another Terrorist Cause

Unfortunately, the ongoing Iraq war has become another terrorist cause. The Brookings Institution's Daniel Benjamin notes that the Iraq invasion "gave the jihadists an unmistakable boost. Terrorism is about advancing a narrative and persuading a targeted audience to believe it. Although leading figures in the American administration have often spoken of the terrorists' ideology of hatred, US actions have too often lent inadvertent confirmation to the terrorists' narrative."

He worries that Iraq has created three classes of largely new terrorists—foreigners in Iraq, Iraqi members of al-Qaeda, and local terrorists in other nations, especially in Southeast Asia and Europe. Indeed, research studies in both Israel and Saudi Arabia have found that most of Iraq's terrorists appear to be new recruits not previously part of the jihadist movement, who were drawn by the war to attack Americans.

In sum, Rep. Ron Paul was right: our interventionist foreign policy generates terrorism. Whether one likes his noninterventionist foreign policy proposals (I do) is another question.

But it is time for US officials, including Republican candidates hoping to become the next president, to address the reality that Washington no longer can escape the consequences of its actions. The United States routinely invades, bombs, and sanctions other nations; Washington regularly meddles in other nations, demanding policy changes, promoting electoral outcomes, claiming commercial advantages, and pushing American preferences. However valid these actions, they create grievances and hatreds. And they spark some disgruntled extremists to commit terrorism. This is not a just or fair outcome, especially to the innocent Americans who are attacked. But it is the unfortunate reality.

Just as Paul Wolfowitz explained, almost exactly four years before Rep. Ron Paul was widely criticized for making the same point.

The Iraq War Is a Failure of Strategy, Not Tactics

Benjamin H. Friedman, Harvey M. Sapolsky, and Christopher Preble

Benjamin H. Friedman is a research fellow at the Cato Institute. Harvey M. Sapolsky is a professor of public policy and organization at Massachusetts Institute of Technology. Christopher Preble is director of foreign policy studies at the Cato Institute.

The authors of the following viewpoint disagree with the popular view that the lesson to be learned from the Iraq War is that it could have been won with more troops earlier on and better co-ordination of efforts. Such a view is dangerous, the authors argue. The real lesson, they believe, is that the United States needs a new national security strategy. Getting rid of Saddam Hussein did not take long; however, the administration underestimated the difficulty of establishing a stable democratic government in Iraq. The long-standing enmity among the sectarian factions in Iraq meant that civil war was inevitable following the demise of Saddam Hussein's police state. The George W. Bush administration's goal of state building was doomed in this environment, the authors claim.

Foreign policy specialists and analysts are misreading the lessons of the war in Iraq. The emerging conventional wisdom holds that success could have been achieved with more troops and cooperation among U.S. government agencies, as well as a better counterinsurgency doctrine. To those who share these views, Iraq is not an example of what not to do, but of how not to do it. Their policy proposals aim to reform the national security bureaucracy so that the U.S. will get it right the next time.

Benjamin H. Friedman, Harvey M. Sapolsky, and Christopher Preble, "Learning the Right Lessons from Iraq," *USA Today Magazine*, vol. 136, no. 2756, May 2008, pp. 14–18.

Need for a New National Security Strategy

The near-consensus view is wrong and dangerous. What Iraq demonstrates is a need for a new national security strategy, not better tactics and tools to serve the current one. By insisting that Iraq was the West's to remake, were it not for the Bush Administration's mismanagement, we ignore the limits on U.S. power that the war exposes and, in the process, risk repeating the same mistakes. The popular contention that the Bush Administration's failures and errors in judgment can be attributed to poor planning also is false. There was ample planning for the war, but it conflicted with the President's expectations. To the extent that planning failed, therefore, the lesson to draw is not that the U.S. national security establishment needs better planning, but that it needs better leaders. That problem is solved by elections, not bureaucratic tinkering.

The military gives the U.S. the power to conquer foreign countries, but not the power to run them. Because there are few good reasons to take on missions meant to resuscitate failed governments, terrorism notwithstanding, the most important lesson from the war in Iraq should be a newfound appreciation for the limits of U.S. power. Instead, the experts fear that Iraq will sour Americans on future interventions—that an "Iraq syndrome" will prevent the U.S. from embarking on future state-building missions. To most experts, this syndrome would be dangerous. For even if Iraq is lost, the consensus view says, the war on terrorism will require the U.S. to repair failed states, lest they spawn terrorism.

To analysts who share these views, Iraq is an experiment that teaches Americans lessons about how to manage foreign populations. Based in part on these lessons, Washington is reforming the national security bureaucracy to make it a better servant of a strategy that requires military occupations, state-building, and counterinsurgency operations—what the military calls reconstruction and stabilization. To that end, the

President and Congress have agreed to expand the size of our ground forces in the hope that our next intervention will not fall short of troops. Think tanks across the ideological spectrum are busying themselves with plans to improve the coordination of national security agencies for the next occupation and to prepare diplomats, soldiers, and bureaucrats to staff it. A new state-building office in the State Department draws up plans for ordering various failed or unruly states. An array of defense specialists offer advice on counterinsurgency doctrine and insist that the military services embrace it. The services indicate that they already have done so. Next time, U.S. leaders are forecasting, the Administration will have a national security bureaucracy capable of implementing American policies; in other words, next time the U.S. will get it right.

Deposing Saddam Hussein was relatively simple. Creating a new state to rule Iraq nearly was impossible, at least at a reasonable cost. What prevents stability in Iraq is not American policy, but the absence of a political solution to the communal and sectarian divisions there. The U.S. invasion exposed those rifts, but their repair is beyond America's power. Maybe the U.S. can improve its ability to manage occupations, but the principal lesson Iraq teaches is to avoid them. Not all state-building missions pose the challenges Iraq does, but most of these missions fail, are extremely costly, and corrode American power.

More Boots on the Ground Not the Issue

Perhaps the most common complaint about the occupation of Iraq is that it was undermanned. The idea is that the U.S. military stripped Saddam's Baathist regime of its monopoly on force in Iraq, but failed to fill the resulting power vacuum on account of a lack of troops and willingness to police the country. The result was anarchy. Iraq's tribes and factions within its various ethnic groups armed themselves and became pseudo governments. Some attacked American troops, and some attacked each other. Disputes broke out over real estate, and the prospect of being manhandled by rival militias brought still more insecurity, defensive arming, and attacks meant to serve as self-defense. Beset by violence, the state collapsed, and the idea of a unified, multi-ethnic country faded.

To avoid these outcomes, analysts say, the U.S. should have sent a far larger occupation force than the 150,000 it had in Iraq when Baghdad fell. A better plan would have two or three times that number, at a ratio of 20 security personnel per thousand of the population. Those figures come from a series of studies published by the Rand Corporation, which arrived at a rule-of-thumb for force ratios needed to maintain order based on a historical survey of past occupations.

The idea that more troops could have saved Iraq from violent discord is flawed on several accounts. First, as David Hendrickson and Robert Tucker argue in a paper prepared for the U.S. Army War College, it would have been difficult, if not impossible, for the U.S. to keep several hundred thousand troops in Iraq for long. Although the U.S. could have mustered a force level of 400,000–500,000 troops temporarily, normal rotation schedules would have required the troops to return home after being deployed a year or less. The nation then would have lacked enough replacement forces to maintain even close to the 130,000 it kept on hand for most of the occupation, unless it either wanted to prevent troops from rotating home or rely heavily on National Guard and Reserve units, both politically dicey propositions likely to damage morale.

The more troops sent in initially, the fewer can remain indefinitely. In a conflict that lasts at least three years in a large country such as Iraq, the U.S. cannot maintain a ratio of one soldier or marine for every 50 civilians, even with a significantly larger military.

The second and more fundamental problem with the idea that more boots on the ground would have prevented Iraq's insurgency is that the way troops are employed matters more than their number. History holds examples of small numbers of troops pacifying large populations and large numbers of troops failing to pacify small populations. The 20 troops per 1,000 civilians ratio for policing populations abroad is drawn, in part, from cases such as Bosnia, where the sides accepted the settlement that the troops enforced. There were no insurgents, unlike in Iraq. The difference is between enforcing peace and making it. . . .

Beyond the too-few-troops argument, most critics of the Administration's conduct of the occupation point to two other key decisions—disbanding the army and de-Baathification—as crucial missteps that empowered the insurgency. These decisions, made at the start of L. Paul Bremer's tenure as head of the Coalition Provisional Authority (CPA), deprived Iraq of managers it needed to run its ministries and government-controlled factories and the security personnel that were necessary to help the Americans keep order. More importantly, the orders angered and impoverished Sunni elites and soldiers—many of whom made particularly skilled insurgents. . . .

Planning Not the Problem

It may be that these decisions were crucial to the U.S.'s subsequent failures in Iraq. A more plausible theory, however, says that the Iraqi state was in disrepair before the American invasion and was held together only by the terror of the dictator that the U.S. removed. Saddam's ouster created a competition for power that was likely to be settled by arms, whatever subsequent decisions the occupying authorities made about the army and the Baath. It is not the argument here that those decisions were wise or that they did not aid in the rise of the Sunni insurgency. The point is that those decisions were not necessary conditions for the insurgency to get its legs, given the broad support it enjoyed, especially among Iraq's Sunni population.

Conventional wisdom indicates that these failures and errors in judgment, as well as many others, can be attributed to poor planning. Better plans would have meant a larger invasion force, which would have prevented central authority in Iraq from unraveling. If it had been operating from better plans, the CPA would not have pursued de-Baathification so aggressively, and it would not have let the Iraqi army collapse. It therefore would not have had to rush to stand up a new army and police force in 2003, forces that were wholly unprepared to fight—and if success in Iraq did call for the training of Iraqi troops, a better plan would not immediately have assigned their training to overwhelmed National Guardsmen, but to personnel in the regular Army and Marine Corps.

The first problem with the logic that better planning would have saved Iraq is that the planning for the war was plentiful and reasonably prescient. The difficulty was the willingness to use the plans. The story is well-documented by [Rajiv] Chandrasekaran's *Imperial Life in the Emerald City*, James Fallows' *Blind into Baghdad*, Thomas Ricks' *Fiasco*, and Bob Woodward's *Plan of Attack*. To the extent that planning failed, it was because of the Bush Administration's expectations about the war and what was needed to sell it. The Administration did not entertain plans for a prolonged occupation, and it saw exercises that envisioned one as efforts to undermine the case for War. . . .

Bush Administration Ignored Advice

The CIA prepared two different estimates pertaining to postwar conditions, one warning about what American occupation forces were likely to encounter in Iraq, the other pertaining to developments in the region. Both proved to be prescient, in that they anticipated that the ethnic and sectarian tensions in Iraq would make it difficult to establish a liberal democracy there that then would serve as a model for the region. Yet, when Paul Pillar, at the time the national intelligence officer for the Near East and South Asia, put those estimates to the President and his senior advisors, one of the officials told Pillar: "You just don't see the possibilities; you are too negative."

"It was clear," Pillar explains, "that the Bush Administration would frown on or ignore analysis that called into question a decision to go to war and welcome analysis that supported such a decision." Insufficient planning did not create these happy thoughts or make the President accept them. Accurate information about the likely postwar situation was available—it either was discarded or ignored. Ideology, combined with a healthy dose of wishful thinking and analytical bias, trumped expertise.

Of course, it is the president's job to settle these disputes and embrace the correct policy before the time to act on them arrives. Bush and [then national security adviser Condoleezza] Rice failed in this regard, allowing plans for a short occupation with few ambitions to dominate until the occupation began, and then settling on a longer occupation for which they had not prepared. The President's failure to referee his subordinates, however, is not a structural deficiency in the U.S. government, but a managerial deficiency in the Bush Administration. No amount of bureaucratic rejiggering can make the president listen to the right people.

The more important problem with the idea that planning could have saved Iraq is that it implies that proper organizational charts and meetings can stabilize broken countries and make order where there is none. This confuses a process with a policy, a bureaucratic mechanism with power. Planning solves engineering problems. Upgrading electrical grids, extending modern sewerage, and rebuilding schools and hospitals—these things easily are planned. The management of foreign societies is another matter altogether.

It is impossible to label the post-invasion civil strife in Iraq as inevitable or to claim that things could not have gone better. Yet, even the wisest American leader, armed with the best plans, would have struggled to implant a liberal order in which the Iraqi people would cooperate easily with one another in a democratic state. There was not then, and is not now, a plan sufficient to solve Iraq's fundamental dilemma—the lack of popular support within Iraqi society for an equitable division of power. People perceive that there is a lot at stake, and many are willing to fight to achieve their goals.

In government, as political scientist Aaron Wildavsky noted long ago, planning basically is a synonym for politics. That is, planning aims to control future government decisions. However, plans over some government activity are the province of all who have power over it, meaning that there are lots of planners and a lot of plans, most incompatible. When you build a house, there is one set of plans. When you build a nation, there are hundreds—and that is just in your government. The trick in politics is not having the right plans; it is having the power to implement them. In societies occupied by the U.S. military, its power severely is circumscribed. The situation in Iraq, seen in this light, is that, even if the U.S. government had aligned its own plans, various factions had other plans, mostly competing, and their conception of their interests so differed from America's and each others' that there was no unity to be had.

The analysts who say more U.S. planning would have saved Iraq confuse the power to conquer foreign countries with the power to run them. The military gives us the former, but the latter is elusive. Even suppressing political violence is far easier, and requires far less control, than convincing people to form a government and obey its laws. The functioning of a modern state requires the participation of millions of people who show up for work, pay taxes, and so on. People do these things because they believe in a national idea that organizes the state or because they are coerced. In attempting to build foreign nations, the U.S. has been unable to impose a national idea.

Moreover, our liberalism—thankfully—limits America's willingness to run foreign states through sheer terror.

If the U.S. occupies a country where the national identity is intact and simply assists in the management of its institutions and in security, state-building may succeed. Success, though, requires the cooperation of the subject population or a goodly portion of it. That is not something that can be created through planning.

There is much solid evidence that the sectarian differences in Iraq meant that such cooperation was not salvageable after the American invasion. It appears that Iraq was held together—but barely—by Saddam Hussein's brutal police-state tactics. Beneath that penumbra of state terror were irreconcilable ambitions among Sunnis, Shi'ites, Kurds, and various groups therein. These differences were likely to produce civil war in the absence of their forced suppression. Note that this was the logic Pres. George H.W. Bush and then-Secretary of Defense [Dick] Cheney cited as the reason they did not overthrow Saddam Hussein after ejecting Iraq from Kuwait in 1991. Note also that the Future of Iraq Project, often mentioned as a guide to preventing Iraq's implosion, actually shows why it was likely. Whatever their wisdom, the papers lacked an outline of a political settlement among the Iraqis, something that has eluded the various Iraqi governments as well.

Overly Ambitious Goals

The Bush Administration sought ambitious goals in Iraq—democracy and capitalism—but even more modest objectives (such as creating stability and a functional state amid warring people) usually are beyond U.S. capacity. Foreign troops still police Kosovo's ethnic groups, and only physical separation keeps them at peace where there are no troops. Proponents of state-building like now-Secretary of State Rice point to the post-World War II occupations of Germany and Japan as examples to emulate. Yet, these occupations relied on conditions the U.S. military could not recreate in Iraq: wars that shattered the fighting spirit of the people, unified polities, and effective bureaucratic institutions that are capable of restoration.

History is awash in failed states, but only a handful have posed a serious threat to American security. A few civil wars have given impetus to jihadism, but it does not follow that the U.S. should join these conflicts, even in the Middle East. The principal interest the U.S. has in lawless states is to prevent a government from taking power that will give refuge to terrorists aiming to attack our country. The states where such concerns are valid are few. Afghanistan and Iraq are exceptions, not the harbingers of a new reality. American actions since Sept. 11, 2001, should deter governments who might be tempted to make common cause with anti-American terrorists. Preventing terrorists from gaining sanctuary in weak states does not require that the U.S. reinvent its state. The U.S. can accomplish the same goals at considerably lower cost through combinations of local allies, intelligence, air strikes, ground raids, and threat of retaliation.

The best way to promote American security is restraint—a wise and masterly inactivity in the face of most foreign disorder. The U.S. should resurrect the notion that the best way to spread democracy is to model it. American ideology sells itself, especially when it is not introduced at gunpoint or during a lecture to the natives instructing them on how they ought to run their country. Likewise, in the long term, unplanned free trade and the wealth it brings may do more to promote stability abroad than the most careful planning. The assertion of raw U.S. power in foreign countries tends to unify America's enemies and weaken the nation's ideological allies.

The lessons drawn from the war in Iraq need to include caution about the limits of American power in remaking states. Iraq should not become a laboratory to perfect the pro-

cess of doing so. The fetish for planning, interagency cooperation, and counterinsurgency might produce some worthwhile
changes in the national security establishment, but it also
might grease the U.S.'s slide into an imperial era foolishly
foisted on Americans in the name of security. Learning the
right lessons from the experience in Iraq should convince
Americans that preserving U.S. power sometimes requires re-
straining it.

For Further Discussion

1. Barbara Gelb writes that the death of Heller's father when he was a young child shaped his life, giving him a preoccupation with death. How is this concern with death reflected in *Catch-22*?

2. Yossarian's speech at the end of *Catch-22* is controversial, evoking criticism from Norman Podhoretz and Joseph J. Waldmeir that it is at odds with the antiwar sentiments of the rest of the book. Do you agree with these critics? Why do you think Heller has Yossarian voice pro-World War II sentiments?

3. Jeffrey Walsh, Wayne Charles Miller, and Joseph J. Waldmeir analyze *Catch-22* in terms of the history of American war novels. Where do they place it? How would you place it? Why?

4. In an interview with Ken Barnard, Heller says *Catch-22* isn't about World War II, it's about the Vietnam War and the Cold War. What did he mean by this statement?

5. Doug Bandow writes that the United States meddles in the affairs of other nations and that these actions create animosity that has resulted in terrorism. Do you agree with him? Is it ever necessary to intervene in the affairs of another nation? If so, what would some legitimate reasons be for U.S. intervention?

For Further Reading

John Dos Passos, *Three Soldiers*. New York: George H. Doran, 1921.

Jaroslav Hašek, *The Good Soldier Svejk*. Prague: Synek, 1926.

Joseph Heller, *Closing Time: A Novel*. New York: Simon & Schuster, 1994.

————, *God Knows*. New York: Knopf, 1984.

————, *Good as Gold*. New York: Simon & Schuster, 1979.

————, *Something Happened*. New York: Knopf, 1974.

Ernest Hemingway, *A Farewell to Arms*. New York: Charles Scribner's Sons, 1929.

————, *For Whom the Bell Tolls*. New York: Charles Scribner's Sons, 1940.

James Jones, *From Here to Eternity*. New York: Charles Scribner's Sons, 1951.

————, *The Thin Red Line*. New York: Charles Scribner's Sons, 1962.

Norman Mailer, *The Naked and the Dead*. New York: Rinehart, 1948.

John Clark Pratt, *The Laotian Fragments*. New York: Viking, 1974.

Erich Maria Remarque, *All Quiet on the Western Front*. New York: Ballantine, 1929.

Dalton Trumbo, *Johnny Got His Gun*. New York: Lippincott, 1939.

Kurt Vonnegut, *Mother Night*. New York: Fawcett, 1961.

————, *Slaughterhouse Five*. New York: Delacorte, 1969.

Bibliography

Books

Peter Aichinger   *The American Soldier in Fiction, 1880–1963*. Des Moines: Iowa State University Press, 1975.

Jerry H. Bryant   "The War Novel: A Blood-Spattered Utopia." In *The Open Decision*. New York: Free Press, 1970.

Bruce Friedman, ed.   *Black Humor*. New York: Bantam, 1965.

Brenda M. Keegan   *Joseph Heller: A Reference Guide*. Boston: G.K. Hall, 1978.

Robert Merrill   *Joseph Heller*. Boston: Twayne, 1987.

James Nagel, ed.   *Critical Essays on Joseph Heller*. Boston: G.K. Hall, 1984.

Raymond M. Olderman   *Beyond the Waste Land: The American Novel in the Nineteen-Sixties*. New Haven, CT: Yale University Press, 1972.

Sanford Pinsker   *Understanding Joseph Heller*. Columbia: University of South Carolina Press, 1991.

Norman Podhoretz   *World War IV: The Long Struggle Against Islamofascism*. New York: Doubleday, 2007.

Stephen Potts   *From Here to Absurdity: The Moral Battlefields of Joseph Heller.* San Bernardino, CA: Borgo Press, 1995.

Sheldon Rampton   *The Best War Ever: Lies, Damned Lies, and the Mess in Iraq.* New York: Jeremy P. Tarcher/Penguin, 2006.

Vance Ramsey   "From Here to Absurdity: Heller's *Catch-22.*" In *Seven Contemporary Authors: Essays on Cozzens, Miller, West, Golding, Heller, Albee, and Powers.* Ed. Thomas B. Whitbread. Austin: University of Texas Press, 1968.

Thomas E. Ricks   *Fiasco: The American Military Adventure in Iraq, 2003 to 2005.* New York: Penguin, 2006.

Tony Tanner   *City of Words.* New York: Harper, 1971.

Periodicals

John W. Aldridge   "*Catch-22* Twenty-five Years Later," *Michigan Quarterly Review,* Spring 1987.

Andrew J.   "This is Not World War Three—or
Bachevich   Four," *Spectator,* July 22, 2006.

Scott Byrd   "A Separate War: Camp and Black Humor in Recent American Fiction," *Language Quarterly,* Fall/Winter 1968.

Jonathan Chait   "The Flack Gap," *New Republic,* April 23, 2007.

Maureen Dowd	"Toil and Trouble," *New York Times*, April 8, 2008.
John Gray	"A Modest Defence of the President and His Policies of Creative Destruction," *New Statesman*, January 17, 2005.
Beverly Gross	"'Insanity Is Contagious': The Mad World of *Catch-22*," *Centennial Review*, Winter 1982.
Alfred Kazin	"The War Novel from Mailer to Vonnegut," *Saturday Review*, February 6, 1971.
Jean E. Kennard	"Joseph Heller: At War with Absurdity," *MOSAIC*, Spring 1971.
Richard Kostelanetz	"The Point Is That Life Doesn't Have Any Point," *New York Times Book Review*, June 6, 1965.
John M. Muste	"Better to Die Laughing: The War Novels of Joseph Heller and John Ashmead," *Critique*, Fall 1962.
Playboy	"The Playboy Interview: Joseph Heller," June 22, 1975.
George Plimpton	"The Art of Fiction, No. 51: Joseph Heller," *Paris Review*, Winter 1974.
William Saletan	"How Did I Get Iraq Wrong?" *Slate*, March 19, 2008. www.slate.com.

Eric Solomon   "From Christ to Flanders to *Catch-22*: An Approach to War Fiction," *Texas Studies in Literature and Language*, Spring 1969.

J.P. Stern   "War and the Comic Muse: *The Good Soldier Schweik* and *Catch-22*," *Comparative Literature*, Summer 1968.

Dan Welch   "Oil and Empire—the Backstory to the Invasion of Iraq," *Peakist*, June 15, 2006. www.thepeakist.com.

Index